Butterfly Valley

For Abdu –

a bilingual edition
hopefully you'll find it beautiful
& inspiring

Sherko Bekas
Butterfly Valley

Translated & introduced by
Choman Hardi

With a Preface by
Gérard Chaliand

love Jude xx.

Arc
PUBLICATIONS
2018

Published by Arc Publications
Nanholme Mill, Shaw Wood Road
Todmorden, OL14 6DA, UK
www.arcpublications.co.uk

Design by Tony Ward
Printed by Lightning Source

978 1911469 07 0 (pbk)
978 1911469 08 7 (pbk)
978 1911469 09 4 (ebk)

Cover picture:
Daro Ola © 2009
Places of Remembrance No. 9, untitled ,
mixed media on canvas, by kind permission of the artist.

This book has been selected to receive financial assistance from
English PEN's 'PEN Translates' programme, supported by Arts
Council England. PEN exists to promote literature and our
understanding of it, to uphold writers' freedoms around the world, to
campaign against the persecution and imprisonment of writers for
stating their views, and to promote the friendly
co-operation of writers and the free exchange of ideas.
www.englishpen.org

Arc Publications Translations series
Series Editor: Jean Boase-Beier

TRANSLATOR'S ACKNOWLEDGEMENTS

Acknowledgements are due to the editors of *Between the Languages* (Modern Poetry in Translation, 2005) and *Wherever I lie is Your Bed* (Two Lines: World Writing in Translation, 2009) where excerpts from an earlier version of *Butterfly Valley* first appeared.

I am grateful for the feedback and support of friends and translators who looked at different sections of this book such as Karen Leeder, George Szirtes, Moniza Alvi, and Dean Parkin. Special thanks to Mimi Khalvati who read the whole of this manuscript and gave me overall feedback. I am indebted to the late Richard McKane who provided invaluable and detailed feedback on some sections and responded to the poem with compassion and sensitivity. Thanks to Azad Berzinji for making available the original Kurdish text and to Ergin Opengin who checked the footnotes and provided the Kurdish transliteration of the names. This book would not be possible without all your contributions.

Most of all, thanks to Sherko Bekas for this beautiful and moving poem which I have lived with for many years. I wish he was alive today to see the book finally published.

Choman Hardi

Sherko Bekas has written a beautiful poem, at once epic and nonetheless sensitive, on the subject of the numerous tragedies experienced by the Kurdish people over the course of the twentieth century. With a gentle touch and certain rhythm, devoid of any melodramatic flair, he recalls the dramatic events that marked the end of the war between Iran and Iraq. The Kurdish minorities in both countries fought against the state upon which they depended, and on both sides found themselves in a difficult position at the war's end. In Iraq, they were made to suffer the vengeance of Saddam Hussein, who resorted to an immense massacre and destruction of hundreds of mountain villages so as to supervise and punish any prospect of resistance from that point onward. All of this is related without laboured tone, like the litany of a wake in which are told, one by one, the beads of a rosary. Halabja certainly recalls the tranquil cruelty of a regime that, in that very location, left five thousand dead, adding to the one hundred and fifty thousand whose demise was most apparently provoked by an exemplary repression that was intended to discourage any ulterior resistance.

This is a very beautiful dirge in which power arises from restraint, and the author speaks as a bard from eras past, recounting to his audience a tale of woe.

A number of other themes are equally conjured, such as the gripping beauty of mountain landscapes, which acted as a refuge of the Kurds who never ceded to defeat, endlessly committing themselves to new uprisings in an effort to tear liberty from the denying hands of their neighbours. As dramatic as they, this poem brims with hope.

Gérard Chaliand
Translated by Nathalie Demirdjian

Contemporary Kurdish poetry is more elaborate and impassioned than English. The abundant use of metaphors, abstract and surreal images, and complex sentences, makes translation difficult at times. In a land where beauty and tragedy intertwine, victimhood and agency exist side by side, devastating events take place without causing a stir in the world, and the difference in temperature between the harsh winters and blazing summers can be as much as 50 degrees, poetry has to live up to and reflect these extreme conditions of life.

Sherko Bekas was a pioneer in Kurdish poetry. Despite his difficult imagery and language, his poetry has been extremely popular. In the 1980s Bekas established himself as the poet of resistance and became the face of the liberation movement. After 1992, when the Kurdistan Regional Government was founded, he focused on broader social justice issues, standing up to religious extremism as well as corruption and nepotism amongst yesterday's revolutionaries. He gave voice to the poor, the women, the marginalised "others".

Bekas' book length poem, *Butterfly Valley* (Derbendî Pepûle), was his fifth poetry book. It was published in 1991 in Sweden, where he had sought refuge. The poem was written in the wake of the Anfal genocide (February-September 1988) and the gassing of Halabja (16th March 1988). Saddam Hussain punished the village population for their support of the liberation movement throughout the 1980s. Two thousand villages were destroyed during Anfal, 281 chemical attacks were launched, and a hundred thousand civilians were exterminated (Hardi, 2011). The attack on Halabja, where five thousand people were murdered, remains the most well known gas attack on civilians in Kurdistan. This is partly because of the large number of casualties but also because Halabja was a town, not one of the villages that were redlined for destruction by Anfal.

Both Anfal and Halabja are central to *Butterfly Valley*. Early on in the poem, Bekas evokes Halabja by speaking of the "doomed spring" and "the frost of March." He expresses yearning to go home and embrace the victims: "the lemon-tree of their figures / poisoned in March." The extremity of the tragedy makes it impossible for Bekas to have a unified and simple reaction. It is impossible to grieve in the usual way.

He mourns the gassing of Halabja through a mixture of conflicting traditions such as folksong, traditional funeral lamentation, and wedding rituals. It is as if the victims are mourned, celebrated, and wed at the same time:

> (Heyran heyrana... that is Seher,
> those are Seher's fallen eyes,
> that is the autumn of Seher's body,
> those are the stray beads of Seher's dreams,
> here are the hands, fingers and breasts
> left behind by Seher,
> those are Seher's rooting screams,
> these are the ashes of Seher's paternal home,
> Heyran heyrana,
> it is hen-night.
> Aman amana,
> it is dancing.)

The former Iraqi state used a cocktail of deadly gasses in the chemical weapons. The gas looked brown and yellow. Some survivors report that it smelt of garlic while others say it smelt of rotten apples. Bekas personifies the chemical weapons into a "a mad air-prince of modernism – / a mixed-race wind, mixed from the left and right politics / of this fallen world, / a wind, large boned, ugly and arrogant/ his mouth smelling of garlic". This prince, according to Bekas, "started a yellow coup." Bekas holds the whole world responsible for the gassing of Halabja, from its East to its West, from its right-wing to its left-wing politics:

> to the brilliant scientists of Pushkin's country, Jack London's country,
> Byron's country, Jeanne d'Arc's country, Bismarck's country!
> The country of Garibaldi, the country of Van Gogh... the country
> of... the country of...
> Thank you for the present, which you sent via Baghdad,
> on the morning of 16th March 1988,
> to the flowers, doves, children and poetry of Kurdistan.

Language fails Bekas. He admits that his "dictionary is limited / under the weight of pain and torture." Words cannot express his pain, they are no longer tools of communication. In Halabja absurdity and contradiction reach a level that they threaten our conceptual framework, threaten coherence and meaning when everything turns into its opposite:

Ogre spring,
cruel flowers,
blind sun,
black snow,
suffocated wind,
rough river,
dry, hard rain,
cold flames, yellow blood,
deaf waves,
dumb explosion.

During Anfal the attacks on the villages continued until every single village was levelled, all water sources were destroyed, the farms were burnt down, animals and farming machinery were looted, and the population was captured. The pain of these events distorts Bekas' sentences and scenes. Normality is a luxury that has been destroyed. In this genocidal atmosphere "knives rain in the wind," "blood flows / from the stone's cave-wound," and "the sound of gushing blood / reaches the ears of history." The large scale destruction creates confusion and chaos such that abstract and material things – humans, animals, and inanimate objects – are confused with each other:

– Is this poetry's left behind locks
or the forelock of a village's dream?
Is this a sun-ray's broken mirror or a girl's?
And this murdered river
was she a field's beloved or a boy's?
And this fallen scream
was it my mother's scream or a tree's?
Is this a nipple or a cherry stone?
Is this a burnt cat or my baby?
Is this my father's head or the bread-pad?
Are these an angel's fallen wings or a dove's?
Are these my irises or olives and grapes?

The poet doesn't know "how to separate them from each other." The world has become surreal, deformed and messed up by destruction, and Bekas mourns with every inch of his body and soul. He feels that he has no choice, the only thing he can do is to write: "You had to do this / to write poetry with the tip of flame / and set fire to your fear and silence."

Memories don't leave Bekas alone. Every day, uninvited and without permission, "a cloud", "a wave", "an oak tree" "a boulder", "a mountain-top," "a river" enters his space, brings him presents, and turns him into "a grove of poetry." His solitude is "brimming" with sounds and images from his past. At times his homeland is so close to him that "there is no distance" between Bekas and Kurdistan. He remembers the villages ("muddy to the neck and wearing shabby clothes") that were targeted by Anfal. He recalls how they provided refuge and shelter to the revolutionaries ("fugitive from my city's streets"). They were the reason the revolution survived:

> they made us nan-bread
> from the dough-ball of their own poverty.
> They covered us with their perforated night,
> made shadows for us with their tree-like figures.

He also gives voice to the ambivalent situation the villagers lived in. Although most of them supported the revolution they were also burdened by it: "they were the coughing mules / under our weapons' weight." He remembers a day when, after a long and thirsty journey over the mountains, he arrives at a village with a group of peshmarga, hoping to be welcomed. Instead, a grieved woman, who is leaking milk, confronts them. She has just lost her husband and baby in a bombardment and she is angry with these revolutionaries:

> What is left for you to come for? The sieve of our bodies?
> Or bloody bread?
> What is left? What have you come for?
> Keep your weapons to yourselves!
> Keep your revolution to yourselves!
> Keep Kurdistan to yourselves!
> What is left? What have you come for?

He remembers the shame he felt, the grief that silenced him and made him turn around, and take the same road back to where he had come from. In another scene, in April, as the Anfal attacks are ongoing, he writes about another village woman who is carrying "her blazed village in her heart." The woman has gone mad and wonders if "God may be on fire." She runs and talks to the smoke:

> You may be the cheerful soul of Uncle Bayiz's stick,
> the spindle of Granny Rehan
> slowly turning around yourself.
> You, smoke of my labour!
> On the forehead of this carefree sky

what are you writing for me?
How many burnt hopes and springs
do I have time to read about?
Who shall I take as witness
to the blazing of my life?

Bekas is enraged by the world's silence towards these atrocities: "Every time, I roll the mountain of screams and sighs/ into the silent ocean of the world/but it does not stir." He knows why so much evidence of extermination and genocide is being ignored. He says, in the voice of "a political barrel of oil": "'If a gallon of my voice stirs / the ocean of the world's conscience will stir with it.'" The world's interest in this region is reduced to oil, nothing else seems to evoke a reaction from the international community.

Butterfly Valley laments the repetitive cycles of Kurdish history (continuous oppression and suppressed revolutions). Bekas imagines meeting Refiq Hilmi, the journalist and historian of the early-twentieth century, who was known for desperately trying to change the course of events, and securing Kurdish independence, while recording them. Sherko Bekas wants to show that, from a political point of view, his generation are in exactly the same position as Hilmi's, only "our pain/ spoke purer Kurdish". When Hilmi shows him the pages of the newspaper he is working on, Bekas responds: "We, too, / have the same hope, the same wound, only our printer is newer, / it is colour and offset."

Exile is another major theme in *Butterfly Valley*. Longing for homeland starts Bekas on a constant search for reminders of it. He tours Stockholm, walks in its rain and sun, throws himself at the wind, follows girls, and circles the markets hoping that an image, a sound, a sensation would briefly take him back to his homeland. He tries to answer the question "What is exile?" by providing various examples until, at the end, he gives up because once again, language fails him and he cannot explain what he feels:

Distress has stretched the wings of my exile,
the threads of my irises have lost focus.
From this distance when I look at my homeland:
every memory, every place,
every dream before the eyes of my memory
become two, become three

become ten... become...
What shall I tell you?
What shall I tell you?
What?

Bekas' pursuit of a political identity in his 1980s exile is futile. It will be decades before people in the West know where Kurdistan is. He describes, in detail, his desperate attempt to explain where he comes from by telling stories and referring to maps ("crumpled like politics, / torn and dirty like the ethics of nation states.") Once a young woman, who is half Moroccan and half Norwegian, tells him that, just like her own father, Bekas is "still having colourful daydreams," and that his "hope is a mirage." This young woman represents the different concerns of the second generation of migrants who view their parents' hopes and aspirations as mirage and daydreams. Bekas fears that his own daughter, who is growing up in exile, will become the same. He fears that one day she too will tell others:

My father was a mountain bird.
He flew the mountain
and reached the snow of this pole.
One day here, as he was singing
his dreams froze with him!

Throughout *Butterfly Valley*, Bekas remembers and speaks to Nali[i], the famous nineteenth-century poet who ended up in Istanbul. While portraying Nali's loneliness in the face of uncontrollable political turmoil, he is in fact addressing his own similar helplessness. He represents Nali riding "the coast-less boat" of solitude, facing the "dark waters" with only "the paddle of his pen." Nali is "conducting the ballad / of stateless waves." Bekas imagines Nali's plunge in social status in the new country. Istanbul where Nali lives, and by extension Stockholm where Bekas lives, do not know who these poets are and what treasure they are to their people. The pigeons see Nali and don't

---

[i] Nali is a famous 19th-century poet born in the Sharazur region of Sulaimani, who migrated to Syrian and then to Turkey. After the fall of the Baban emirate in Sulaimani, he spent the rest of his life in Istanbul. It is believed that he passed away in 1855. He was the first poet who started writing in the old version of the Sorani dialect spoken by Bekas.

know "what fine wings / lay in that blue soul's sky." The sunset doesn't know "what ember, flame and fire burn / in the hearth of that exiled and wandering poem." The rain doesn't know "what roar, labour, motion, and thunder / linger in that deep mind's cloud." Similarly, people pass by Bekas without knowing or caring about who he is and where he comes from.

At the end of *Butterfly Valley*, Bekas sets the stage for meeting Nali, "the king of exiles." They will meet "by the shore / of the sad pond" nearby. He tells us about the presents he will give to Nali, the kind of things they will talk about, how they will exchange grief, poems, longing. He tells us that this is the night when his dream will come true, he will meet Nali, and together they will go home to their beloved city, their Hebiba.

Bekas' complex poetic language, together with various references to historical Kurdish events, personalities, and geographic locations, make understanding his poetry difficult for non-Kurds. Many personalities are evoked in this poem, from the poets (Nali, Haji, Mewlawi, Goran) to the revolutionary leaders (Sheikh Mahmud, Khendan), religious leaders (Mewlana), historians (Hilmi), journalists (Jeladat), and famous lovers (Braimok, Las and Khezal). Often, places, mountains, and fields near where these personalities lived are connected to them in the poem. For example, in 'Haji's Kekon', Kekon is a hill near Koysinjaq where the poet, Haji, comes from.

This translation has been a lengthy and complicated process but despite the difficulties I have tremendously enjoyed working on *Butterfly Valley*. Sherko Bekas has a few book-length poems but *Butterfly Valley* remains my favourite. This book evokes exile, flight, political persecution, and Kurdish history better than any other book I know. For the sake of not overwhelming the reader with too much detail, we decided to cut down some of the more difficult sections in this poem. What comes to you in this book is 70% of the original poem. When I first heard a tape recording of this poem in 1991, even without seeing the book, I fell in love with this poem and memorised parts of it. I hope that English readers can learn to appreciate Bekas' craft and enjoy *Butterfly Valley* as it deserves.

Choman Hardi

15

Butterfly Valley

دڵۆپ، دڵۆپ باران: گوڵ ئەنووسێتەوەو
ئە ئەیش چاوانم تۆ!.
چ ساڵۆینێکی[1] نامۆیی و چ ژانێکی بەخشندەیە
وا لەسەرخۆ
بەرد بە بەردی
کێوی سەرم ئەپشکوێنن
لق بە لق و چڵ بە چڵی
دەست و پەنجەی وشکەڵاتووم
شین ئەکەن و وەک باویلکە[2]
ئەمدەن بە دەم بارێزرەکەی ئەوینتەوەو
لەشەختە بەندانی گیانتا: ئەمرسکێنن.

گڤە، گڤە "با" پێدەشتت ئەخوێنێتەوەو
نەفەس نەفەس هەناسەیشم: باڵاکەی تۆ
چ گەردەلوولێکی سەوزەو
چ ئەسپێکی ئەفسانەیی باڵدارە وا
لەم کۆتایی دنیایەوە
بە پرتاو دێ و هەڵم ئەگرێ و ئەمفرێنێ و
دوور دوور ئەمبا
بەرەو هۆبەی ئارانی[3] تۆ.

کلوو، کلوو بەفر گوێ بۆ چیا ڕائەدێرێ و
وشە وشەیش هۆنراوەی من بۆ سۆزی تۆ
چ بەفرانبارێکی زەردە و
چ کڕێوەی حیکایەتێ بەم ناوەختەو
لە ئاویلکەی[4] ئەم ڕۆژەدا
وەک عەشقەکەی "برایمۆک"
پێدەشت پێدەشت و کۆ بە کۆ
بە ڕێگەی مەرگی سپیدا
ئەمخاتە ڕێ بەرەو لای تۆ

* * *

سەفەرە
سەفەرە
سەفەر.

---

[1] ساڵۆ: ساڵێک ئاوی زۆربێ
[2] باویلکە: گیایەکی تووک سپییە لە پایزاندا با بڵاوی ئەکاتەوە.
[3] ئاران: جێی زستانەی کۆچەران.
[4] ئاویلکە: وەختی گیانداران.

Drop by drop the rain writes flowers
as tear by tear my eyes compose you.
What streaming year of exile, what generous pain,
which bring to blossom the mountain of my head,
stone by stone;
branch by branch and twig by twig,
they germinate my parched hands, my fingers,
and like thistledown they surrender me
to the wind of your love,
to sprout in the frost of your soul.

Crackling and rustling the wind reads fields
and gasp by gasp, my breath calls on you.
What is this green hurricane,
this legendary winged horse,
speeding to snatch me
from this end of the world,
to carry me to your nomads,
their winter quarters!

Flake by flake, snow listens to the mountain
and word by word, my poems attend to your love.
What is this yellow snowfall,
this blizzard of an untimely story
which in the death throes of today
propels me towards you
field by field, mountain by mountain,
along the path of a white death!

    * * *

It is a journey,
a journey,
journey,

سەفەری ئازاری زگماک و سەفەری
درەختی بێ دالّدە و بێدرێتەی [5] زامانی گەریدەو
تەدارەك رێك ئەخەم!
ساواقە [6]
ساواقە
ساواق!
ساواقی سالّانەی بەهاری بێولّەت
ساواقی بورجی "مارت".
شەپۆری باهۆزە و شیوەنی گولّانەو
تەدارەك رێك ئەخەم
تەدارەك: لە ئەسپی كەلّلە سەر گرگرتوی رەوەندم
ئەو وەختەی ژان لەسەر بەرد ئەروێ.
تەدارەك لە حیلەی بروسكەی ئەم هەورە سوورانە
ئەو دەمەی كە باران شیعرێكی سەوزتر ئەنووسێ.
لە جوانووی ئەم خەمە بزێوە سپیانە
ئەو وەختەی كە لانكە و بنچك و
دەوەنیش غار ئەكەن.
تەدارەك لە تەختی كەژاوەی زریكەی فەریادی
ئەم هەموو فریشتە رەندانە
ئەو وەختەی خوا ئەوقەو
مردنیش سەرسامە!
لەگوارە و پلّپلّەو سلّسلّەی زایەلّەم
ئەو دەمەی كە شایی گریانە.
تەدارەك لە تاری ئەم شیعرەو
گەردانەی ئەم تەمە
ئەو وەختەی كە مەرگم بووكمە و
كەژەهریش شاباشی جیهانە!

ئێوارە.. دوای بانگی برینتان من ئەگەم.. ئێوارە.
ئێوارە.. دوای شێوی گریاوتان لاتانم.. ئێوارە.
كە هاتم
مۆمێكم لە قوللەی حەزرەتی "نالیی"دا بۆ هەلّكەن
با ملی داری بێ
یان پەنجەی نێرگزێ
یان قژی وەنەوشە.
زامێكم لە دوندی "كەكۆن" [7] ی "حاجی"دا بۆ پێكەن

[5] بێرێتە: سەمای بەكۆمەلّ.
[6] ساواق: سەرماو سۆلّەی سەختی دژوار.
[7] كەكۆن: گردێكە لە رۆژئاوای راستە كۆیەی جاران.

the journey of inherent pain,
a homeless tree's journey,
the ensemble of wandering wounds,
so I prepare myself.
It is a frost,
a frost,
frost,
a yearly frost of the doomed spring,
the frost of March.
It is lamenting windstorm and sobbing flowers,
so I prepare myself.
When pain blossoms on stone
I prepare my horse, his head blazing for departure.
When rain writes a greener poem
I prepare these red clouds' whinnying thunder.
When the cradle, the shrubs,
and the bush gallop
I prepare these white sorrows' restive colt.
When God is astonished
and death perplexed
I prepare the palanquin of pretty angels
screaming for help.
When weeping rejoices
I prepare my clattering lamentations.
When death is my bride
and poison is the world's gift
I prepare this poem's veil,
this mist's necklace.

Twilight, after your wounds' summon I arrive, twilight.
Twilight, after your weeping dinner, I will be with you, twilight.
Light me a candle in saint Nali's[1] summit when I arrive.
Let it be a tree's neck,
the finger of a narcissus, or wisteria's tress.
Light me a wound on the peak of Haji's[2] Kekon[3],

[1] Nali (in Kurdish: Nalî) is a famous 19th century poet born in the Sharazur region of Sulaimani who migrated to Syria, then to Turkey. After the fall of the Baban emirate in Sulaimani, he spent the rest of his life in Istanbul. It is believed that he passed away in 1855.
[2] Haji Qadiri Koyee (in Kurdish: Hacî Qadirî Koyî) was a poet from Koysinjaq.
[3] Kekon mountain is near Koysinjaq.

با سەری بڕڕاوی شیعریّ بیّ
یان مەمکی "وەسانان"[8]
یان بالّای هەلّەبجه.
دوای بانگی برینتان من ئەگەم.

[...]

تاکوو دیّم، ئەو گولّه سپیانه مەنیّژن
بوەستن! بەلانکەی میّژوویان مەسپیّرن
با لەسەر سەوزەگیای لەشی هەرد
لەسەر پشت پالّکەون
با لەسەر باسکی ئاو راکشیّن
با لەسەر شانی "با" هەلّکوڕمیّن.
ئاسمانی چاویشیان دامەخەن
هیچ پەلّه هەووریّکی سەرشاخیان
پیا مەدەن، هەتا دیّم
مەیکەنه تاروومار
خۆزگەمه بۆ دواجار
تەماشام به پرژەی گولّاویان تەڕ بکەم.
خۆزگەمه بۆ دواجار
شنەیان بگرمه باوەشم.
یەك به یەك دەم خەمه ناو دەمی حەسرەتیان
ناکامیی سینەیان هەلّمژم
وەك دایك و
باران و
شەمامه
بۆنیان کەم.
یەك به یەك دەست بیّنم
به تیشك و تیریّژی قژیانداو
موو به موو ماچیان کەم.

تاکوو دیّم، ئەو "مانگ"ە زەردانه مەنیّژن
بوەستن! هەتاکوو تریفەی غەریبیی خۆم دیّنم
راوەستن! هەتاکوو ئەگەم و
خەرمانەی هەلّبەستم
ئەکەمه پشتیّنی ناو قەدیان.
خۆزگەمه بۆ دواجار
دەست کەمه قەلّبەزەی گەردنی هەمووویان

---

[8] وەسانان: گوندی "شیّخ وەسانان"ی هەریّمی هەولیّر لەلایەن رژیّمی عیّراقەوه ژەهرباران کرا.

let it be a poem's decapitated head,
Wasanan's[4] breast,
or Halabja's figure.
After your wounds' summon, I arrive.

[...]

Don't bury those white flowers till I come.
Wait! Don't give them up to the cradle of history.
Let them lie on their backs
on the grass hill,
let them rest on the water's forearm,
let them lean on the wind's shoulder.
Don't close the sky of their eyes,
don't cover them with a mountain cloud, till I come,
don't disperse them.
I wish, for the last time,
to wet my eyes with the sprinkle of their perfume.
I wish, for the last time,
to embrace their breeze,
to put my lips on their desires' lips, one by one,
to breathe in their disappointment,
to smell them
like mother,
rain,
and muskmelon,
to pass my fingers
through the beams of their hair
and kiss them strand by strand.

Don't bury those yellow moons till I come.
Wait till I bring my exile's moonlight.
Allow me to arrive
so I can harvest my poems
and make a belt for their waists.
I wish, for the last time,
to embrace the rapids of their necks,

---

[4] Wasanan (in Kurdish: Wesanan) is a region in Kurdistan which was
chemically bombarded in 1987 and 1988.

یەك بە یەك خەمانیان راژەنم
یەك بە یەك بە بەژنی دار لیمۆی ژەهراوییی
مارتیاندا هەڵزنێم
یەك بە یەك سەرخەمە ناو سنگ و بەرۆکی بەفرینیان
یەك بە یەك کرنووشیان بۆ بەرم
یەك بە یەك فوو بکەم
بە کونی زامیاندا و
شمشاڵی باڵایان لێ بدەم:

(حەیران.. حەیرانە.. ئەوە "سەحەر"ە
ئەوە چاوی هەڵوەریوی سەحەرە.
ئەوە خەزانی باڵای سەحەرە.
ئەوە دەنکە ملوانکەی خەونەکانی سەحەرە.
ئەوە دەست و ئەوە پەنجە و ئەوە مەمکی
بەجێماوی سەحەرە.
ئەوە قیژەی رواوی سەحەرە
ئەوە خۆڵەمێشی ماڵە بابی سەحەرە
حەیران حەیرانەو
خەنە بەندانەو
ئامان ئامانەو
باڵا رێزانە..)

[...]

ئەوەیان: فەنەری گەردنی "نالیی"یە لە شەوی
"بسفۆر"دا[9] ئەسووتێ و جەستەی ئاو ئاڵ ئەکات.
بە باڵای قەسیدە قوڵایی ئەپێوێ و لە بنی گێژاودا
چارۆگەی خەیاڵی هەڵئەدا. لە سامی گێژەوندا و
لەوێدا بۆ ساتێ پەیتووکەی[10] گومانی ئەسرەوێ. لەوێدا
ئەم گەرای رەنگاڵە بۆ ماسیی باڵداری شیعری خۆی
دائەنێ. لەوێدا ئەم خەونی زەرد و سوور بە چاوی
خاکەوە ئەبینێ. ئەخنکێ و ناخنکێ و لەوێدا دەست ئەباو
مرواریی دڵی خوا دەردێنێ. ئەخنکێ و ناخنکێ و
لەوێدا ئەم تۆوی هەتاو و هۆنراوە ئەچێنێ. هەر خۆی و
گەمیەکەی. هەر خۆی و سەفەری ئاوی رەش.

_____

[9] بسفۆر: دەریای بسفۆر.
[10] پەیتووکە: چۆلەکەی بچووکی تیژباڵ و خێرا.

24

to rock their sorrows, one by one,
to climb, one by one,
the lemon-tree of their figures
poisoned in March,
to put my head on their snowy chests, one by one,
to bow to them, one by one,
to blow into their open wounds
and play the flute of their bodies, one by one:

(Heyran Heyrana[5]... that is Sahar[6],
those are Sahar's fallen eyes,
that is the autumn of Sahar's body,
those are the stray beads of Sahar's dreams,
here are the hands, fingers and breasts
left behind by Sahar,
those are Sahar's rooting screams,
these are the ashes of Sahar's paternal home,
Hayran hayrana,
it is hen-night.
Aman amana,
it is dancing.)

[...]

That is the candle of Nali's neck burning
in the pacific ocean's night, brightening the water's body.
He measures the sea's depth by the epic's length, sails his dreams
at the bottom of the whirlpool. Stunned by the whirling
the hummingbird of his fear rests for a second. Over there
he lays colourful eggs for his poetry's winged fish.
Over there, he has vivid dreams about his homeland's eyes.
He is about to drown when he reaches out
and extracts the pearl of God's heart. He is about to drown
when he plants the seeds of sun and poetry. It is just him
and his boat, him and the journey of dark waters,

[5] Heyran is a particular kind of folksong which is a very long love
story and involves singing and talking.
[6] Sahar (in Kurdish: Seher) is a woman's name, it also means dawn.
This is referring to a sad love song about the insomnia and grief of
the lover when the beloved has deserted him.

هەر خۆی و سەوڵەکەی قەڵەمی و هەر خۆی و خەمی

گەش. پێشەنگە و پێش هۆرەی شەپۆلی بێ وڵات

کەوتووە. پێش وشەی سەرگەردان کەوتووە.

نامۆیی سەراپای تەڕ بووە.

بەلەمی بێ کەنار

تەنیایی ئەئاژوێ و

باخی ئاو

گوڵ قژی "حەبیبە"ی گرتووە.

[…]

"ئەستەمووڵ" ئەیبینێ و نازانێ چ گۆمێ

وا لە ژێر کڵاوی ئەم پیاوە

ڕیش ڕەشە ڕێحانە و بەفرەدا.

هەموو ڕۆژ ئەیبینێ و نازانێ

چ بێشەو نزارێ وان لەناو

دەربەندی ئەو سینه تەنگەدا.

کۆتریی سەر قوببە و مناره ئەیبینن نازانن

چ باڵی فڕینێ وا لە ناو ئاسمانی

ئەو گیانە شینەدا.

کەلەپوّی[11] خۆرنشین ئەیبینێ و نازانێ

چ پشکۆ و ژیلەمۆ و ئاگرێ وان لەناو

ئاتەشگەی ئەم شیعرە ئاوارە و وێڵەدا.

باران و ڕەهێڵە ئەیگاتێ و نازانێ،

چ ناڵەو چ ژان و ژمژیە[12] و گرمەیەک

وان لەناو ئەو هەوری دەروونه قووڵەدا

هەژاران ئەیبینن نازانن

چ نووزەی نانێک و چ لاڵەی ئاوێ و

چ سەرمای تەمەنێ وان لە ناو

کوختەکەی هەناوی

ئەم مامه پیرەدا!!

عاشقان بەلایدا ئەڕۆن و نازانن

چ لەنجەی خەمێک و

چ کانیی نیگایەک

وان لەناو کازیوەی ئەو چاوە تیژەدا.

[…]

---

[11] کەلەپوّ: ئەو کەلەی خۆری لێئاوا ئەبێ.

[12] ژمژیە: جوڵان و بزوتنەوە.

him and the paddle of his pen, just him and the bright
sorrows. He is the pioneer, conducting the ballad
of stateless waves. He leads the wandering words.
Exile is soaked.
The coast-less boat rides solitude
and the water's garden
has blossomed Habiba's[7] hair flowers.

[...]

Istanbul sees him and doesn't know what lake
laps beneath this man's hat,
with his basil and snow beard.
It sees him every day and doesn't know
what grove and shadows
rest within that tight chest's valley.
The pigeons of the minarets and domes
see him and don't know what fine wings
lie in that blue soul's sky.
The sunset mountain sees him and doesn't know
what ember, flame and fire burn
in the hearth of that exiled and wandering poem.
The rain and showers reach him and don't know
what roar, labour, motion, and thunder
linger in that deep mind's cloud.
The poor see him and don't know
what begging bread, gasping water
and coldness of a lifetime hide
in the cottage of this old man's soul.
The lovers pass him by and don't know
what swaying sorrow
and what spring of vision
are in the dawn of those sharp eyes.

[...]

[7] Habiba (in Kurdish: Hebîba) was Nali's beloved whom he never
married. He has composed many poems about her.

درێژە دووکەڵی ئەم بێشە غەمناکە
وەک بەژنی نەخشەکەم.
درێژە فرمێسکی ئەم شاخ و داخانە
لە دیجلە و فوراتیش درێژتر.
درێژە کرووزەی پەلکە گیا
تا چاوی برینم بڕ ئەکا.
درێژە هاواری کۆڵان و شەقامی ئەم لەشە
تا لای خوا.
درێژە ئازاری ئەلف و بێم
لێرەوە هەتاکوو لای "خانیی".
درێژە، درێژە.. درێژە.. غەریبیم
لە هێڵی ئاسنی ئەوروپا درێژتر.
نازانم ئەز چیتان بۆ باسکەم؟
نازانم ئەزچیتان
نازانم ئەز
نازانم
نا.
وا دیسان خەنجەرە و بە "با"وە ئەبارێ.
ڕەهێڵەی نەشتەرە.
شادەمار لە ملی ئەم کێوە زلەدا
کون بووەو خوێن لەبەر
ئەشکەوتی برینی بەرد ئەڕوا.
وا دیسان چەقۆیە و بە "با"وە ئەبارێ

"با" سەرم ئەبات و
گیانیشم بە دوایدا ئەگەڕێ.
- پێویست بوو، شاخ بێتە، دەشتایی گیانتەوە.

پێویست بوو کڵاوی هەووری ئەو لە سەرکەیت.
ئەبوایە تان و پۆی پەنجەی تۆ و لاسکی گژوگیا و
فەقیانەی دایکت و تەنافی سێدارە تێک ئالێن.
پێویست بوو بە قەڵەم سەنگەریش لە شیعرا هەڵکەنی.
ئەبوایە خوێ و برین وەک عەشقی وەلی و شەم،
وەک سەری مەسیح و تاجی دڕک، پێکەوە ڕابێنی.
پێویست بوو ئەو کاتەی شڵپەی خوێن لە ڕۆخی
لەشەوە، ئەگەیشتە گوێی مێژوو، لەو زەریا

Long is the smoke of this grieved grove
like the figure of my map.
Long are the tears of these mountains and valleys,
longer than Tigris and Euphrates.
Long is the smouldering of a blade of grass
as far as my wound's vision goes.
Long are the screams of this body's roads and streets,
they reach God.
Long is the pain of my alphabet
from here till Khani[8].
It is long, it is long, it is long… my exile
longer than Europe's rail track.
I don't know what to tell you about
I don't know what
I don't know
I don't.
Once more knives rain in the wind,
it is the storm of lancets.
The artery in that mountain's neck
has slit and blood flows
from the stone's cave-wound.
Once more knives rain in the wind.
The storm takes my head
and my soul searches for it.
'It is essential for the mountain to enter your body's field,
for you to wear its cloud's hat.
It is essential that your fingers and the stems,
your mother's sleeves and the hanging ropes, entangle.
It is essential that your pen digs trenches in poetry,
that you habituate salt to wounds like Weli's[9] love to Shem[10],
like Christ's head to the crown of thorns.
When the sound of gushing blood
reaches the ears of history

[8] Ahmed-i Khani (in Kurdish: Ehmedê Xanî) is a 17th century
Kurdish poet known for his verse romance *Mn and Zin*.
[9] Weli Dewana (in Kurdish: Welî Dêwane), Weli The Mad, was a poet
whose famous poem *Shemi Sheman* (in Kurdish: Şemî Şewan) (Night's
Candle) became a classic song.
[10] Shem (in Kurdish: Şem) is a Persian word meaning candle, which
is how Weli Dewana referred to his lover. There is a theory that her
name was Shemsa.

سووڕەدا، ئەبوایە چارۆگەی بەلەمی دەنگی خۆت
هەلبکەی. چی ئەکەی؟ ئەو کاتەی کە مردن
سەربازی دەولەت بێ و تۆیش لە کێو، درەختی
قەلەم بی؟ چی ئەکەی ئەو وەختەی کە شانۆت
پەنگربێ و گوێ گرت تفەنگ بێ؟
– هەر ئەبوو، وابکەی، هۆنراوە
بە نووکی بلێسە بنووسی و
دۆزەخیش بۆ ترس و بێ دەنگیت دابخەی!

– بەردەوام هەر تەورە و بە "با"وە ئەباری.
بەردەوام لافاوی شمشێرە و هێرشی بیابان.

* * *

– ئەمە پرچی بەجێماوی قەسیدەیە؟
یان کاکۆلی خەونی گوندێ؟
ئەمە ئاوێنەی شکاوی هەتاوێکە
یان هی کچنێ؟
ئەی ئەم ڕووبارە کوژراوە
یاری دەشت بوو یان هی کوڕێ؟
ئەی ئەم قیژە هەلوەریوە
قیژەی دایکمە یان درەختێ؟
ئەی ئەمەیان گۆی مەمکە یان دەنکە گێلاس؟
ئەمە پشیلەی سووتاوە یان ساواکەم؟
ئەی ئەمەیان سەری باوکمە یان گولبێنەی تەندوورەکە؟
ئەمانە بالی وەریووی پەریەکانن یان کۆترەکان؟
ئەی ئەمانە گلێنەمن یان دەنکە زەیتوون و ترێ؟
نازانم ئەز چۆنیان لە یەکتر جیاوەکەم؟
نازانم ئەز چۆنیان لە یەکتر
نازانم ئەز چۆنیان..
نازانم ئەز.
نازانم..
نا..

[…]

it is necessary to sail your voice's ship in that red sea.
What else can you do, when death is the state's soldier
and you are a pen-tree in the mountains?
What else can you do, when your stage is ember
and your audience is rifle?'
'You had to do this –
to write poetry with the tip of flame
and set fire to your fear and silence.'

Axes keep raining in the wind,
the swords storm and the desert assaults.

    * * *

– Is this poetry's left behind locks
or the forelock of a village's dream?
Is this a sun-ray's broken mirror or a girl's?
And this murdered river
was she a field's beloved or a boy's?
And this fallen scream
was it my mother's scream or a tree's?
Is this a nipple or a cherry stone?
Is this a burnt cat or my baby?
Is this my father's head or the bread-pad?
Are these an angel's fallen wings or a dove's?
Are these my irises or olives and grapes?
I don't know how to separate them from each other,
I don't know how to separate
I don't know how to
I don't know how
I don't know
I don't.

    [...]

هەموو جار بێ ئەوەی لە دەرگای وشەم بات

هەورێ دێ

خۆی ئەکا بە ژوورمـا و گۆرانیی قژ تەڕم بۆ دێنێ

بێ ژوان

بەبێ پرس

هەموو ڕۆژ

شەپۆلێ، دووان و سیان،

بە هەگبەی پرشنگ و گوڵەوە

ئەگەنه سێبەری بەرگێلەم[13]

نارۆن تا من نەکەن بە مێرگی هۆنراوەو

بە گۆمی ئەستێرەیش ژوورەکەم.

دار بەرِوو دێ بۆ لام

رِەگی خۆی ئەبەستێ بە رِەگی قاچمەوە.

گابەرد دێ و هێزی خۆی

بەدیاریی بۆ پشتم ئەهێنێ.

لوتکه دێ و باڵای خۆی

ئەخاتە سەر باڵام.

ئاشنامن فرمێسکە پایزەی غەریبان

ئەوانیش بە سواری کزەبای

ئێواران دێن بۆ لام.

[...]

هەر لێرەم. دەمێک بوو ئەو گونده

تا پشت مل قوراوییی و کوڵنجه شرانه.

ئەو خەمه دەست و پل زبرانەی وڵاتم

بازۆڵەی ئازادیی و، بۆ هەزار، هەزاران

سروودی ڕاکردووی شەقامی شارانم لانکەبوون.

دەمێک بوو چۆڕچووورِەی ئارەقی لاملی

گەنم و جۆی ماندووویان

بۆ رِێچکه ئەستێرەی سەر هەوراز، دەوران دەور،

بۆ رِەوە برینی خۆ خۆریش، ئەوان هەر

نیگایان پلوسکی بەفراوی کاوان و

ئارامییان کاسه دۆی ئەوینی سەر رِێ بوو.

دەوران دەور، دەمێک بوو، ئەوانه هەر هەڵمی

گوڵاوی رِەنج بوون و ژەم بە ژەم:

---

[13] بەرگێله: هەیوانی بەردەم شاخ و رِەوەزو ئەشکەوت.

Every time, without knocking on my words' gate,
a cloud comes along, enters my room
and brings me wet-haired songs.
Every day, without an appointment,
without permission,
a wave, or two or three
reach the shadow of my porch:
their luggage full of moonlight and blossom.
They don't leave until they turn me into a grove of poetry
and my room into a lake of stars.
The oak tree comes to me
and ties its roots to the roots of my feet.
The boulder comes and presents
its strength to my back.
The mountain-top comes and adds
its height to mine.
Exile's autumn tears are my acquaintance,
they too, riding the evenings' chilled wind,
come to me.

[...]

I am still here. For a long time those villages,
muddy to the neck and wearing shabby clothes –
those sorrows with calloused hands and feet,
were freedom's embrace and a cradle
for thousands and thousands of hymns,
fugitive from my city's streets.
For a long time, the dribbling sweat
from their tired wheat-and-barley's necks,
was reviving snow-water
and a loving mug of *dogh*
serving lines of stars in the mountains
and even the self-destructive flocks of wounds.[11]
For a long time they were
the rosewater of anguish and every meal

---

[11] Referring to internal war between the Kurdish parties, the civil war, during the revolution. This was happening in the 1970s and 1980s while at the same time they were all fighting the Baath regime together.

له گوونکی هەژاریی خۆیانیان بۆ کردین و نان و
له شەوی کون کونی خۆیانیان پیادەین و
بەڕیزه درەختی باڵایان سێبەریان بۆ کردین.
ئەو گونده دەم و چاو خۆڵاویی و پێپەتی و رووتانه
باوەشیان کادان بوو
قسەیان باسووق و
مندا‏ڵیان رێواس و
گەورەیان پەل و پۆی دار شاتووی ناو دێ بوون.
دەوران دەور
ئەوانه هەر پرمەی ئێستری سەر پلەی
ژێر باری تفەنگی ئێمه بوون.
دەوران دەور
ئەوان هەر: هێلکه بوون، کەشکبوون.
پێوازبوون بۆ ژیان
ئەوان هەر: خرخاڵ و بازن بوون بۆ شیعر و
چیرۆك بوون بۆ کوانووی نیشتمان!

[...]

ـ له بیرته؟ ئەو ساڵه نەزۆکه
به بزنه رێیەکی بێ ئاوی نیوەڕۆی هاوین‌دا ئەرۆیشتی
تفەنگی سەرشانت سێبەری تینویەتی و
تابووتی مەرگێکی گەرۆك بوو.
بۆ ئێوه، بۆ ئەوان، هەموو‌شت تارمایی
ترسێکی هەمیشه ئامادەی درێژ و، بەرین بوو.
داروبەرد، ئاژەڵ و باڵدار و، هەتاکوو
بریسکەی چاوانی پشیله‌یش له شەودا، بۆ هەموو
نیشانەی بانگدانی مردن و نێو فاقەی کەمین بوو.
بەشاخی ماندوو‌دا داگەرای.
چووی‌ته ناو برینی گوندەوه:
ئەو، که هات دار هەرمێی سەرتاپا رەشپۆش بوو.
ئەو، بۆنی مەرگێکی زۆر تازەی لێ ئەهات.

ژنێ بوو له مێژووی زامداری شاخ ئەچوو.
ئەو، سەری مێردەکەی له سنگیا نیشاندای
ئەو، شیری گریاوی ساواکەی بۆ هێنای
پێی وتی:
ـ بۆ هاتووی؟
چی ماوه تا بۆی بێن؟ بێژنگی لاشەمان؟!

34

they made us nan-bread
from the dough of their own poverty.
They covered us with their perforated night,
made shadows for us with their tree-like figures.
The embrace of these dusty-faced, barefoot and naked villages
was our barn,
the villagers' conversations were our sweet Basooq[12],
their children were rhubarbs,
their elders were the mulberry tree's stems and branches.
They were the coughing mules
under our weapons' weight.
They were eggs, cheese and onion
for our lives.
They were anklets and bangles for poetry,
stories for homeland's hearth.

[...]

– Do you remember? That sterile year
you walked the waterless summer afternoon track.
The weapon on your shoulder was thirst's shadow
and a migrating death's coffin.
For you, for them, everything was the ghost
of a permanently ready fear, long and wide.
Sticks and stones, animals and birds, and even
the glittering eyes of a cat in the night
were the signs of death's call and ambush for everyone.
You descended the exhausted mountain
and entered the wound of the village:
When she came, she was a mourning pear tree.
She smelled of a new death.

She looked like the mountain's sorrowful history.
She showed you her husband's picture on her breast.
She brought you the crying milk of her baby.
She told you:
– Why have you come?
What is left for you to come for? The sieve of our bodies?

---

[12] (In Kurdish: Basûq) A type of sweet made from grapes and
walnuts.

یان نانی خوێناوی؟!

چی ماوە بۆ هاتووی؟!

تفەنگتان بۆ خۆتان!

شۆڕشتان بۆ خۆتان!

کوردستان بۆ خۆتان!!

چی ماوە بۆ هاتووی؟!

شەلاڵی شەرمێکی گەرم بووی. ئەو وەختەی وەرچەرخای

مردبووی!، بە هەمان بزنە ڕێی تینوودا

بە هەمان سەرشاخی ماندوودا سەرکەوتی

لە ملەی پێشتەوە

باگژەی،[14] ڕقاوی، بە هەڵپەی تەپ و تۆز هەڵیکرد

تەندووورەی گەردەلوول گەیشتە بەردەمت و

تیا ون بووی!

* * *

هەر لێرەیش بوولێڵی[15] دوێنێ بوو

من خۆم دیم "بە پەلە مێژوو هات، بە خۆی و

چەند ڕەوە ئەسپەوە -وەك بڵێی ساڵێکی

ون بووبێ و بە دوایدا بگەڕێ -من خۆم دیم

پەشۆکاو. داستان هات، بە خۆی و چەند ڕەوە بروەسکە و

هەوورەوە -وەك بڵێی هەواڵی کوژرانی "ئەنکیدۆ"

یان کاوەی بیستبێ. ئەو وەختەی خۆیان کرد بە دەرگای

زیوینی دەربەندا، هەر هەموو ئەسپەکان، سوارەکان،

سەرتاپا هەڵمێکی زەرکەفتیی لە لەشیان هەڵ ئەستا.

چیایان شڵەژان، درەخت و تاڤگە و ڕووباریان سەرسام کرد.

تاریکی نزاریان شڵەقان. سوارەکان: ڕم بوون و،

تا ناو قەد تڵەتڵ[16] ئەسووتان، بەگوێی خۆم گوێم لێبوو،

لوتکەکان بەیەک دەنگ بانگیان کرد "وا شێخ هات"[17].

ئەم چرا یاخیانە، سەروڕیش پرشنگی ئاڵۆزکاو، بازوویان

ڕووبار و تەوێڵیان ئاوێنەی بناری بەرھەتاو.

14 باگژە: نێوان ڕەشەباو کزەبا.

15 بوولێڵ: سەرەتای شەو. تاریکایی دوای ئێوارە.

16 تڵەتڵ: گڕو بڵێسەی ئاگر.

17 واشێخ هات: مەبەست شێخ مەحمودی نەمرە.

Or bloody bread?
What is left? What have you come for?
Keep your weapons to yourselves!
Keep your revolution to yourselves!
Keep Kurdistan to yourselves!
What is left? What have you come for?

You were drenched in hot shame. When you turned back
you were dead! You took the same thirsty track back.
You climbed the same exhausted mountain
and from the front the wind was angry,
it started with force, raised dust.
The whirlwind's oven reached you
and you got lost in it!

* * *

Yesterday's darkness dwells here.
I saw it myself, history came in a rush
with herds of horses – as if it had lost a year
and was looking for it. I saw it myself,
fable came all distressed, with its flock of thunder
and clouds – as if it had just received the news of Enkido's[13]
or Kawa's[14] death. When they entered
the valley's silver gate, gold steam was rising
from the horses, the horsemen.
They shook the mountains, puzzled the trees, waterfalls, rivers.
They stirred the shadow of the mountainside. The horsemen
were piercing spears, ablaze down to their waists.
I heard it with my own ears, the mountain peaks
called out together 'Sheikh is here!'[15]

The beards of these rebelling lanterns were entangled rays,
their arms were the river and their foreheads mirrors in the sun.

[13] In the epic story of Gelgamesh, Enkido is Gelgamesh's best friend.
[14] According to an old legend, Kawa was the brave blacksmith who killed
Dehak, a brutal Assyrian king, on the 21 March (the Kurdish and Persian
new year), and built a large fire on the mountain to inform the public.
[15] Sheikh Mahmud Barzinji (in Kurdish: Şêx Mehmûd) was the leader of a
series of Kurdish revolts against the British Mandate of Iraq, demanding
Kurdish independence.

خۆم بینیم بەم هەردوو چاوانە: لە دەفەی شانیاندا
قوڵە قوڵ ئازادیی هەڵئەقوڵیی، خۆم بینیم: لە وەردو
نواڵەی سنگیاندا گوڵاڵە ڕواوە، خۆم بینیم بەم هەردوو
چاوانە: هەرەیەکە و ڕۆحی خۆی کردووە بە چەپک و،
چەپکیشیان هەر لەسەر قەڵپووزی زینەکان داناوە.
خۆم بینیم: هەر یەکە و دوا قومی مەتارەی سوێندێکی
قرمزیی لەگەڵ خۆی هێناوە.
ئەسپەکان: ڕەنگاوڕەنگ سپی و ڕەش، بۆڕ، سپی،
قاوەیی، ئەسپێکیان باڵدار بوو ڕەنگی شین.
گۆمێ بوو ئەیحیلان. ئەم ئەسپە شینەیان،
کە باڵی لێک ئەدا بە جارێ ڕەوە ئەسپ کورژنیان ئەکرد و
ڕەوەزیش ئەکەوتنە سمکۆڵاڵن. ئەو وەختەی باڵیشی
جووت ئەکرد، زریانیش وەک شەختە ئەمەیی.
پێشوازیی لەشکری باوبۆران، پێشوازیی ئەم خێڵی
ئاگر و کلێپەیە، تا دەرەنگ خایاندی، نیوەشەو لە بەردەم
ئەشکەوتی (جاسەنە)[18] دابەزین. جلەوی شۆڕشمان
لێگرتن. ماچ. گوڵ و پەپوولە و گەنم بوون ئەبارین.
هەردوولا وەک دوو چەم تێکەڵ بووین. هەموومان
هەر هەمان دەم و چاو. هەموومان ناومان (لاس)
هەموومان هەر بە شوێن گوڵەکەی خەزاڵدا ئەگەڕاین.
زمانمان گۆڕیەوە هەریەک بووین،
خەفەتمان گۆڕیەوە هەریەک بووین.
هەر تەنها پۆشاکی برینمان یەک نەبوو.
لەو هاڕاو زۆنگەدا، خولیام بوو، من "حیلمی"[19] ببینم.
پرسم کرد. شیعرێ هات: ستونیی، ئاماژەی بۆ کردم
دوور بە دوور کەپرەکەی نیشاندام. چووم بۆ لای،
کە من چووم خەریکی نووسینی هاواری ئازارو خەمێکی
درێژبوو، بۆ یەکەم لاپەڕەی "بانگی هەق"[20]، دانیشتم.
خەمەکەی دامە دەست، لێم وەرگرت، سەیرم کرد
هەر هەمان هاوارە، هەر هەمان ئازارە، کە ئێمەیش
هەر ئەمڕۆ دابوومان بە ڕادیۆی ئەم شاخە -ئازاری

[18] جاسەنە: گوندی جاسەنەو ئەشکەوتی جاسەنە لە ناوچەی سورداشی سەر هەرێمی سلێمانی.
[19] حیلمی: ڕەفیق حیلمی، ڕووناکبیرو مێژوونووسی سیاسی ناوداری کورد.
[20] بانگی هەق: ڕۆژنامەی (بانگی هەق)ی شۆڕشی شێخ مەحمودی نەمر. ماوەیەک ئەم ڕۆژنامەیە لە ئەشکەوتی جاسەنە دەرئەکرا.

I saw it with my own eyes: beat on beat, freedom surged
from their shoulder-blades. I saw it: red poppies grew
on the spread of their chests. I saw it with my own
eyes: each had made their soul a bunch of flowers
laid out on their saddles' pommel.
I saw it: each of them had brought with them
the last sip from their red oath's flask.
The horses were colourful: black, white, piebald,
brown, one was blue and winged.
This blue one was a neighing lake,
when he flapped his wings the herd neighed
and the boulders would start pawing.
And when his wings gathered, the high wind froze.
Greeting this army of wind and rain, greeting this tribe
of fire and flame, took a long time. By midnight
they dismounted before the Jasene[16] cave. We took the bridle
of revolution from them. Kisses rained like flowers, butterflies and wheat.
We mixed with them like two river streams. All of us
had the same face. We were all called Las[17],
all looking for the flower, Khezal.
We exchanged our times and we were the same,
we exchanged our sorrows and we were still the same.
Only the garments of our wounds were different.
In the crowd of voices, I was longing to meet Hilmi[18],
I asked after him. A vertical poem came and pointed faraway,
to his hut. I went to him.
When I arrived he was busy writing a long sorrow
for the first page of *Bangi Heq*[19], I sat down.
He gave me his sorrow, I took it, looked at it,
it was the same cry, the same pain, which we had broadcast
on the mountain radio that day – our pain

---

[16] Jasene Cave (in Kurdish: Casene), near the city of Sulaimany, is where
the Bangi Haq (in Kurdish: Bangî Heq) paper was published by Sheikh
Mahmud, during the British occupation.
[17] Las and Khezal (in Kurdish: Xezal) were two famous lovers, like
Romeo and Juliet, who never united.
[18] Refiq Hilmi was a historian and journalist who became advisor to
Sheikh Mahmud and later founded the Hiwa Party.
[19] *Bangi Heq* (in Kurdish: Bangî Heq) was the first Kurdish paper in Iraq,
published by Sheik Mahmud, fighting for independence under British
occupation.

لای ئێمه کوردیهکهی پهتی تر نووسیبوو.- پاش تۆزێ
بردمی "چاپخانهی ئاوات" و برینی نیشاندام. که بینیم
پێکهنیم -چاپهکه پیرێ بوو دهست شکاو پهککهوته.
من پێم وت:
مامۆستا! ببوره لای ئێمهیش
ههر ههمان ئاوات و برینه
ئهوهنده، چاپهکهی لای ئێمه تازهیه و
ڕهنگاوڕهنگ ئۆفسێته!!

[...]

– له نێوان وشهی تۆ و کانیدا جودایی نهماوه.
لهنێوان قهڵهمت و لاسکدا جودایی نهماوه.
لهنێوان دهروونت و ئاگرا جودایی نهماوه.
لهنێوان نهفهست و ههوادا جودایی نهماوه.
تۆ ئیسته، کهنیسمهی، سهرتاشه بهردێکی مێژوویت و
به خوێندن بهژنی "با" سوور ئهکهیت. تۆ بهباڵ
ئهبینی و به چاوت کیشوهری ئهم سۆزه تهی ئهکهیت
که گهڵا بکوژرێ ناتوانی دهنووکت کلیل بهی.
تۆ ملت ژێی خاکه و دهستی ئاو ئهتژهنێ.
که ئاوێك کوێر بکرێ ناتوانی پهنجهرهی شهتاوت
دابخهی. تۆ یاڵی ئهم ئهسپی کهژانهی. که جوانووی
شهماڵێك سهربهرن ناتوانی قهت حیلهی سنجرت[21]
خهفهکهی.

ده ههگبهی بارانی هۆنراوهت بکه شان!
له ڕێگهی گوڵهوه بچۆره ناو خێڵی
ڕووناکی و دهستکهره گهردنی دارستان.
ده ههگبهی گۆرانی و گوڵاڵهت ههڵگرهو
له ڕێگهی ئاوهوه بچۆره ناو دهنگی
خهڵکهوهو سهربده له وهرزی سووتان و ههڵقرچان.

ههموو جار به خوررهم دات ئهکرد
سهرتاپای کهژاوهی ئهو ههموو گوندانهت تهرئهکرد!

– ههنووکه شهوو ڕۆژ گوێ ئهگرم له لاڵیی
ئهستێره و گوڵهباخ.
لهلاڵیی دهربهند و دارستان.
له کپی و بێدهنگیی کاولاش و خۆڵهمێش.

––––––––––
[21] سنجرت: بڵێسهی ئاگر.

40

spoke purer Kurdish. After a while he took me,
showed me the publishing house of hope and wounds.
When I saw it, I smiled – the printer was a disabled old man –
I told him: Apologies, Sir! We, too,
have the same hope, the same wound,
only our printer is newer,
it is colour and offset.

[...]

"There is no distance between your words and the spring.
Between your pen and the stems,
your soul and fire,
your breath and air,
there is no distance left.
Now you are a lark on history's rock
reddening the wind's height with your song. You see
with your wings and you travel your love's country with your eyes.
You cannot lock your beak when a leaf is killed.
Your throat is land's string and the water's hands play you.
You cannot shut your waves' windows when they blind water.
You are the mane of these mountain horses,
you cannot extinguish your flames' neigh
when they behead a breeze's colt.

So take the bag of your raining poems,
enter the light's tribe through the flowers' path
and embrace the forest's neck.
So take the bag of your songs and poppies,
enter the people's voice through the water's path
and visit the season of burning and blazing.

Every time when you poured down
the palanquin of all the villages got soaked."

– Now I listen to muteness day and night,
the muteness of stars and roses,
the muteness of valleys and forests,
to the silence and stillness of ruins and ashes.

هەنووکە من لەگەڵ مێژووی کەڕ ئەدوێم و
زمانم غەریبی فەرهەنگی خۆیەتی و
دەنگیشم مەلێکی گرمۆڵەی بێ ئاسمان.

چۆڵ و هۆڵ پێ دەشت و بناری ئەم لەشە دروێنە کراوە
چۆڵ و هۆڵ پایتەختی ئەم شیعرە خنکاوە.
چۆڵ و هۆڵ وڵاتی ئەم خەونە سووتاوە.
چۆڵ و هۆڵ، چۆڵ و هۆڵ
لەم سەری زامەوە هەتاکوو ئەو سەری.
لەم پەڕی کۆستەوە هەتاکوو ئەوپەڕی.

تۆ فریا نەکەوتی ئاوەکە بەیتە دەس "مەولەوی".
تۆ فریا نەکەوتی کەوشەکان بۆ "ناڵیی"ی دابنێی.
تۆ فریا نەکەوتی کەوچکێ دەرمان بەیت بە "گۆڕان"
تۆ فریا نەکەوتی و نەکەوتی و نەکەوتی.

لە جێی خۆت خەزان بووی، بێ ئەوەی هەڵوەرێی.
لەجێی خۆت هەڵقرچای. بێ ئەوەی بشێوێی.
لە جێی خۆت بووی بە مۆم. بێ ئەوەی بسوتێی.

(بروسکەیەك.. پەلەنییە.. شیعریش نییە.)
بەناوی هەڵەبجە و پێنج هەزار (مانگ)ەوە
بەناوی مەولەوی و پێنج هەزار گوڵەوە.
بەناوی گۆڕان و پێنج هەزار کۆترەوە،
بۆ زانا بلیمەتەکانی: وڵاتی پوشکین، وڵاتی جاك لندن.
وڵاتی بایرۆن، وڵاتی جان دارك، وڵاتی بسمارك.
وڵاتی گاریباڵدی، وڵاتی ڤان کوخ.. وڵاتی.. وڵاتی.. وڵاتی
سوپاس بۆ ئەو دیاریيەی کە بە کۆمەڵ سەر لەبەیانی رۆژی 16/3/1988 لە رێگەی بەغداوە بۆ گوڵ
و کۆتر و منداڵ و شیعری کوردستانتان ناردبوو.

[...]

- سەرەتای نیسان بوو، ژنێکی لادێی
گوندەکەی بە گروکڵپەوە خستبووە ناو دڵی و رای ئەکرد
وەکوو دار، وەکوو بەرد، وەکوو ئاو

42

Now I converse with a deaf history,
my tongue is a stranger to its own dictionary,
my voice is a hunched, skyless bird.

Deserted are this harvested body's fields and valleys.
Deserted is this smothered poem's capital.
Deserted is this burnt dream's country.
Deserted, deserted –
from this side of the wound to the other,
from this side of the catastrophe to the other.

You did not have time to pour Mewlewi[20] a sip of water.
You did not have time to give Nali his shoes.
You did not have time to offer Goran[21] a spoon of medicine.
You did not have time…. did not have time… did not have time.

You were autumn in your own place, without falling.
You blazed in your own place, without shifting.
You became a candle in your own place, without burning.

(A message which is not rushed, neither is it poetry):

In the name of Halabja and five thousand moons.
In the name of Mewlewi and five thousand flowers.
In the name of Goran and five thousand doves,
to the brilliant scientists of Pushkin's country, Jack London's country,
Byron's country, Jeanne d'Arc's country, Bismarck's country!
The country of Garibaldi, the country of Van Gogh… the country
    of… the country of…
Thank you for the present, which you sent via Baghdad,
on the morning of 16th March 1988,
to the flowers, doves, children and poetry of Kurdistan.

    […]

– It was the beginning of April. A village woman
was running, carrying her blazed village in her heart.
Like the tree, stone and water

[20] Famous poet of the Hawrami dialect.
[21] Founder of modern Kurdish poetry.

شێت بووبوو:

"دووکەڵ، دووکەڵ، دووکەڵ..
رەنگە خوا سووتابێ و ئەم هەموو دووکەڵە
لەو هەڵسێ!"
ڕای ئەکرد وای ئەوت.

"ئەی دووکەڵی بەژنی دایکم
لە وەختی نزاکردندا!
ئەی دووکەڵی بەژنی مێژووم
لەوەختی هەتاو چاندندا!
تۆ ڕۆحی سەوزی گژوگیا و دارستان و
کێڵگە فریوەکانی ئێمەی بە دەوری
ئەم شاخانەدا خول ئەخۆی.
تۆ باخ و مەزرا باڵگرتووەکانی ئێمەی
سەرت ناوە بە بنمیچی تاریکیی کەشکەڵانەوە.
تۆ گیانی سپی بێشکە و پنە و بەرماڵ و
حیکایەتی گوێ ئاگردانی ئێمە بووی
ئەوا ئیستا بە ئاسمانەوە پەرت ئەبی.
تۆ گیانی سەرخۆشی ڕەزەکانی ئێمەی
واقاچت لە دوت نایەن و سەرسم ئەدەی.
ئەی دووکەڵی خەوەکانم!
تۆ ڕەنگە ڕۆحی قۆشمەی گۆچانەکەی مام "بایز"و
تەشیەکەی نەنە "ڕێحان"بی
وا لەسەر خۆ هەڵ ئەسوورێیت و با ئەخۆی.
ئەی دووکەڵی ڕەنجەکانم!
لەسەر ناوچەوانی گرژی
ئەم ئاسمانە بێ باکە چیم بۆ ئەنووسیت؟!
من ئەتوانم فریای خوێندنەوەی چەند هیواو
بەهاری سووتاو بکەوم؟!
من کێ بکەم بە شایەتی
ئەم هەڵقرچانەی ژیانم؟!

– تۆ زەردەشتێکی سووتاوی
ئەوەتە هەی گڕ ئەتخوات و هەر گڕ ئەگری
ئەوەتە هەی ئەم جیهانەیش
ئاسمانێکی کوێرووکەرەو
تۆیش بەردەوام هەر دووکەڵی!

[...]

44

she had gone mad:
'Smoke, smoke, smoke…
God may be on fire
this smoke may be rising from him!'
She was running and saying:
'You, smoke of my mother's figure at prayer!
You, smoke of my history's figure
while planting suns!
You are our forests' green soul,
our flown fields,
circulating around the mountain.
You are our winged farms and gardens
rubbing your head against the dark milky-way.
You are the white soul of our cradle, bread and prayer mat.
You are our bedtime stories by the fire,
now dispersing in the sky.
You are our vineyards' drunken soul,
now stumbling, your feet not following you.
You, smoke of my dreams!
You may be the cheerful soul of Uncle Bayiz's stick,
the spindle of Granny Rehan
slowly turning around yourself.
You, smoke of my labour!
On the forehead of this carefree sky
what are you writing for me?
How many burnt hopes and springs
do I have time to read about?
Who shall I take as witness
to the blazing of my life?'

– You are a burnt Zoroaster.
Flames have been eating you all your life
and you keep burning.
All your life this world has been
a deaf and mute sky
and you are always smoke!

    […]

– لەسەر ئەم تاوێری ئاواتە، وەستاوی.
ئەزانی جاربەجار ئەلەقێ و وەستاوی.
"بوەستە! هیوایەك بشلّەقێ
لە قوللەی چەسپاوی تاریکیی چاکترە تیا بژیت"
ئەم پەندە
دووکەلّی شەرابیی
ئەو هەموو ڕەزانە بۆی نووسیت!

هەموو جار من کێوێ هاوار و زریکە
تلاوتل ئەبەم و ئەیخەمە ناو زەریای
بێدەنگی دنیاو.. ناشلّەقێ.
هەموو جار من سەری بڕراوی سالێکم، شارێکم
هەلّ ئەگرم ئەیبەمە بەردەمی
بۆ ئەوەی بپرسێ
ئەم سەرەت لە کوێوە هێناوە؟!
ناپرسێ

– "گالّۆنێ لە دەنگم بشلّەقێ
ئەم زەریای ویژدانی جیهانەیش
لەگەلّیا ئەشلّەقێ"
ئەم پەندە
بەرمیلە نەوتێکی سیاسی بۆی نووسیم!

– "هەر لەبەر نەزانیی سوار نییە
ئەم شاخە هەموجار ئەگلێ.
دارخورمای خواستراوی "سوریا"
لە "بەردەقارەمان" سوارترربوو؟!
ئەم کێوە بە تەنها و بەسکی برسی هەر
ئەوەندە غار ئەکا!"

[...]

لە عومری شاخەوە مشاری زەمانێ نەماوە
سەرنەکا بە خوێنی مێژووتا
لە عومری شاخەوە پەیکانی سولّتانێ نەماوە
بە نووکی خۆیەوە ئەم سەرە یاخیەت بانەدا
سولّتان مرد.. بەرد نەمرد!
شمشێر مرد.. با نەمرد!

46

– You are standing on this boulder of hope.
You know it is shaky at times but you are standing.
(Stand as you are! A shaky hope
is better than the stable summit of darkness.)
This advice
was written by the burgundy smoke
from all the vineyards.

Every time, I roll the mountain of screams and sighs
into the silent ocean of the world…
but it does not stir.
Every time, I carry the decapitated head
of one of my years, my cities,
and take it before the world so that it will ask me:
'Where have you brought this head from?'
But it does not ask.

'If a gallon of my voice stirs
the ocean of the world's conscience will stir with it.'
This advice was given to me by a political barrel of oil!

– It is not always because of the horseman's callowness
that this mountain falls every time.
Was the borrowed Syrian date-tree
a better horseman than Berda-Qareman[22]?
This lonely mountain with a hungry stomach
can only gallop this much.

[…]

From the beginning of the mountain's life
there is no saw of an era
which hasn't cut into the blood of your history.
From the beginning of the mountain's life
there is no arrow of a sultan
which has not pierced your rebel head.
The sultan died… the stone didn't.
The sword died… the wind didn't.

[22] This is the large boulder under which Sheikh Mahmud (in Kurdish:
Şêx Mehmûd) hid when he was wounded in a battle with the English.

"منیش نیازمه، ئەم گۆزەیەی سەروملم تێك بەمەوە.
جارێكی دی بیشێلمەوە، لەبەر ئەوەی ماوەیەكە،
ئاوی خەیاڵی لێ ئەچێ. شیعرەكانم فێنك ناكاو،
وشەیشی پێوە ناوەستێ. منیش نیازمه، گردۆڵكەیەكی
چەپكەی ناو دەروونم، بكەم بە گۆڕستانی هەموو
بەرهەمە مردووەكانم. نیازم نییه گۆڕەكانیان
بۆ هەڵبەستم. یاخود لەسەر كێڵەكانیان هیچ
بنووسم. نیازم وایه ئیتر ئەستێرەی یادگار، لە كلۆری
هیچ دارێكی زری خەڵكا نەشارمەوە. نیازم وایه،
من لە ساكۆی ئەم مەرمەری رەشی شەوە، پەیژەی
هەتاو دابتاشم. نیازم وایه بۆ ئەم فرینه تازانه،
ئاسمانی نوێ، شەقڵنی نوێ، بدۆزمەوە.
نیازم وایه، هەرچی هەڵمی دەربدەدەر و ئاوارەیه.
لە شەوێكی ئێجگار ساردا، لە ئاسمانی كوردستاندا
كۆكەمەوە. دواتر كوورەی هەناوی شیعری
نالی یان بۆ دابخەم. هەتا ئەبن بە شەستە
باران و تۆڤ و تێكەڵ بە دایكمان ئەبنەوە.
نیازم وایه خانووویەك بۆ:
شیعری سبەینێ و دواڕۆژم دروست بكەم. وێنەی نەبێ.
"بریتۆن"[22] بە خەو نەهیدیبێ. خانووویەك بێ:
لەقەدپاڵی شەماڵێكی سەوزو سووردا.
بەسەر پێ دەشتی هەوورێكی ئەرخەوانیدا بڕوانێ.
دیوارەكانی مەرمەری تەم و مژبن.
دەرگاكانی لە دار ئەبەنووسی شەوبن.
هەموو پەنجەرەكانی لە:
ئەلەمنیۆمی هەتاوبن.
بە كۆنكرێتی سامالێش بنمیچەكەی داڕێژرابێ.
من ئەگەر بێ و لە خانووویەكی وادا بنووسم
بە زمانی خوایی پەتیی شیعر ئەنووسم
پیتەكانم كلووی بەفر و تەرزە ئەبن.
وشەكانم گڤەی زریان.
قەڵەمم باڵی فریشته و دەفتەریشم شەپۆل ئەبن.
من نیازم نییه لە ژێر ئەم رەشماڵی
شیعرانەدا خەیاڵ پیركەم.
یان هەر لەژێر یەك سایەدا
گوڵەكانم پرچی سپی بهۆننەوە.
رەنگه دوای یەك چركەی تر من
بگوێزمەوە و بڕۆم بچمه وڵاتێكی دیكەی جوانیی.
رەنگه بچمه ئەپارتمانی "رۆمان"ەوە
یان ناو كەشتیی شانۆیەك و
یاخود ئەستێرەی تابلۆیەك

_____
[22] بریتۆن : 'ئدەنری ه بریتۆن' شا ع یری باهونبانگی فەرەنس .

(I intend to dismantle the pottery of my head and shoulders
and remake it once more. It has been dripping
imagination's water. It no longer cools my poetry
nor does it retain my words. I intend to turn an isolated hill
within my soul into a graveyard for my dead work.
I don't intend to give them headstones, nor to write on them.
I intend not to hide the stars of remembrance
in the cavity of people's rotten trees.
I intend to create ladders of light
from the platform of the night's dark marbles.
I intend to find a new sky, new flapping wings
for these new flights.
I intend to gather the wandering and exiled clouds of steam
in a freezing night-sky above Kurdistan
and light the stove of Nali's poems for them
so that they rain and storm and rejoin their motherland.
I intend to build a house
for tomorrow's poems, a house without equal,
a house which Breton hadn't even dreamt of.
A house next to a colourful breeze,
overlooking the field of lavender clouds,
its walls made of marble mists,
its doors made of night's ebony trees,
all its windows made of the sun's aluminium.
Its ceiling made of the clear sky concrete.
If I write in such a house
I will write poems in God's pure language,
the letters will be snow-flakes and hail-stones,
my words will be the rustling wind.
My pen will be the angels' wings
and my notebooks will be waves.
I don't intend to let my imagination age
in the tents of these poems
or allow my flowers to grow grey
under one shadow.
Maybe in a second
I will move house to another country of beauty.
I may go to a novel's apartment,
or a theatre's ship,
or a painting's star,

یان هەر ببم، بە "ئاخ" یەکی ناو گۆرانی و
لە جۆلانەی ئەودا بمرم!"

[...]

لە ئێستا بە دواوە من ئێتر: هەڵەڵەبجەم!
لە ئێستا بە دواوە من دەنکە فرمێسکی هەناری
ئەو خەمە گەورەیەم.
لە ئێستا بە دواوە من باری ئەو سێوەم
کە ئێتر بارناکرێ بۆ ئەوێ.
لە ئێستا بە دواوە من تاڵێ لە ریشی
هۆرەکەی مەولەویم
لە ئێستا بە دواوە ئەو شەمی شەمانی
وڵاتمە و من وەلیم.

پێم بڵێن من چی بکەم بۆ ئەوەی گریانیی کافووریی
ئەم زەڵمەم لووزەوی کەم نەکات؟
پێم بڵێن من چی بکەم بۆ ئەوەی ئەم جوانووە
سەرکەکەشەی هەنیسکم رام نەبێت؟
دەبڵێن من چی بکەم، چی نەکەم؟ بۆ ئەوەی
خوا بێتە خوارەوە و هیچ نەبێ بۆ تاوێ
لە پرسەی ئەم "مانگ"ە جوانەدا
لەگەڵمان دانیشێن؟!
پێم بڵێن من چی بکەم؟
پێم بڵێن من
پێم بڵێن!
پێم.

‌‌‌‌- لەم دەشتەدا، چۆن وا لە پر ئەم بنجکی زریکانە
گوڵیان کردوو بوون بە چواڵە؟!
لەم دەشتەدا، چۆن وا لەپر ئەم گۆرانییە وەریوانە
روانەوە و بوون بە لالە؟!

or I may turn into a sigh in a song
and die in its swing!)

[...]

From now on I am Halabja!
From now on, I am a tear-seed
of that vast sorrow's pomegranate.
From now on I am the load of apples
which won't be caravanned there[23].
From now on I am a strand of hair in the beard
of Mewlewi's song.
From now on he is the *shemi shewan*[24] –
the evening candle of my country,
and I am the infatuated Weli.

Tell me what shall I do so that the camphoric cries
of Zellm Lake do not die down?
Tell me what shall I do so that this obstinate colt of my tears
does not get tamed?
Just tell me, what shall I do? What should I not do?
So that in this pretty moon's wake
God comes down, at least for a short while,
to sit amongst us?
Tell me what shall I do?
tell me what...
tell me...
tell.

– How sudden the bushes of scream in this field
flower and grow into green almonds.
How sudden the fallen songs in this field
germinate and turn into tulips.

[23] Refers to a line in a folk song which says: "The apples have been loaded to go to Halabja".
[24] *Shem* means candle and *shewan* means nights (in Kurdish: Şemî Şewan). Literally Mewlewi says 'Candle of the night' but this refers to his beloved whose name was Shamsa (he called her Sham for short). In this other sense the phrase means 'Shamasa of the nights'.

هەڵەبجە- هەنگێکم ئەچمەوە ناو خەونی منداڵیم
یادگار ئەمژم:
"زەردو سوور حەوت ساڵە خەیاڵم
هاوینە و لەسەربان، نەمامم پاڵ کەوتووم.
درەنگان خۆم ئەکەم بە شوانی ئەستێرە
فەرەنجیم تریفەو
تیزماڵکی²³ هەورێکیش گۆچانم.
مرواری ئەستێرە ئەژمێرم
حەز ئەکەم، خۆزگەمە، ئەو گەشەی سەرپەریان
بۆ ناو چیغ داگرم
وەک تۆپە شینەکەم بیخەمە باخەڵم!
هەڵەبجە ئەمخاتە سەرشانی بەرزی خۆی
قاچێکم ئەلەرزێ، خەریکم بکەووم
بە دەستی چەپ خێرا
توند قژی "شنرۆێ" ئەگرم و
دەستی راست هەڵئەبرم،
– وەک بە رۆژ چۆن هەنار
هەناری "باخی میر"²⁴ ئەدزم ـــ
ئەمشەویش ئاوەها ئەستێرەی سەرلقی
ئەم باخی ساماڵە دائەگرم.
وا ئیستە لە چیغدا ئەستێرەم گرتۆتە باوەشم
لە دەنگی جریوە و جووکەی ئەو، باوکیشم هەڵ ئەسێ
دەست ئەبا و ئەستێرە هەڵئەگرێ
لە نێوان منداڵیی و شیعردا دای ئەنێ
لەم لاوە من ماچی ڕوومەتی زیوینیی ئەکەم و
باوکیشم لەولاوە
شیعرێکی لەبەردا ئەنووسێ!"

"16"ی مارت –"بەر لە نیوەشەوی ئەم رۆژە قرچۆکە
شازادە هەوایەکی مۆدێرنیزمی شێت
هەوایەکی دوو رەگ، لە نەسلی چەپ و راستی
سیاسەتی ئەم دنیا بەستۆکە²⁵.
هەوایەکی کەتەی بەئۆکی²⁶ لەخۆبایی
بۆنی دەم سیراویی.
کوت و پر هات و کودەتایەکی زەردی
ئەلەکترۆنی بەرپاکرد.

---

²³ تیزماڵک: بەشێکی باریک و درێژ لە هەر شتێ.
²⁴ باخی میر: باخی میری ناوداری شاری هەڵەبجە.
²⁵ بەستۆکە: ژنی داوێن پیس.
²⁶ بەئۆک: ناشرین. ناقۆڵا. سامدار.

Halabja – I am a bee returning to my childhood dream,
I suck memories:
(Colourful, my imagination is seven years old.
It is summer and I am lying down on the roof.
Late night I become the stars' shepherd.
Moonlight is my coat,
a stripe of cloud is my stick.
I count the pearls of stars,
wish to pull down the sparkling one
at the beginning of the row
and bring it into my bed
to embrace it like my blue ball!
Halabja stands me on her high shoulders,
my legs shake a little. I am about to fall
when I quickly grasp mount Shinirwe's hair
with my left hand.
I raise my right hand
– just like the days
when I used to steal pomegranates from Mir's garden[25] –
tonight I steal
stars on the stems of this clear-sky's garden.
Now I hug the star in my curtained bed,
my father wakes up from its singing.
He reaches out and picks up the star,
he puts it between childhood and poetry.
From this side I kiss its silvery cheek
and from the other side my father
writes a poem by its light!)

16th March – before mid-day
a mad air-prince of modernism –
a mixed-race wind, mixed from the left and right politics
of this fallen world,
a wind, large boned, ugly and arrogant
his mouth smelling of garlic –
suddenly arrived and started a yellow coup.

---

[25] Mir's (in Kurdish: Mîr) garden belonged to the famous prince (mir) of
Halabja.

دەستی بەسەر تەخت و بەختی ئاسماندا گرت.
بوو بە تاقە فەرمان ڕەوای
ئەم مەملەکەتە بەرینەی بەهار.
ڕێ و بانەکانی هەناسەی نێوان
ئاسمان و زەوی بەست،
تەواوی دەرگاکانی بەهەشتی کڵۆم کرد
بە دەنگی تێکەڵی ڕۆژهەڵات و ڕۆژئاوا
بەیاننامەی ژمارەیەکی خۆی خوێندەوە.
هەر ئەوەندەی لەرینەوەی گەڵایەك و کەمتر.
هەر ئەوەندەی تروکەی چاوی ئاوێك و کەمتر،
هەر ئەوەندەی نووزەی کارژۆلەیەك و کەمتر.
چی فریشتە و حۆری و پەری و باڵدار و بێ باڵ هەبوو
کردنی بەمۆم بێ ئەوەی هەڵیان وەرێنێ.
کردنی بە شووشە بێ ئەوەی بیانشکێنێ
لە کەنار ئاوی ڕەشی ئەم ڕۆژە کپەدا
پۆل پۆل کۆترەکان سپی ئەچوونەوە-
هەر ئەوەبوو نەیان ئەگماند.
لە مەزرا و پاوانە سەوزەکانی ئەم ڕۆژە گێڕووێژەدا
ئەسپەکان ڕەوە ڕەوە پاڵ کەوتبوون
هەر ئەوەبوو نەیان ئەحیلاند.

لەبەردەم ئەم هەوا شێتەدا
کێ ئەتوانێ بە پێوە بوەستێ؟
کێ دەستەوەستان نابێ؟
هەر لە "گاتا"کانی زەردەشتەوە
تا "سەرمایە"ی مارکس
تا شمشێرەکانی "ژواڵفقار"
ڕشانەوە و بڵقیان کرد و خپ بوون.
ئازایەتی، جوامێریی، بیروباوەڕی ئاگرین
لە سەنگەرەکانی خۆیاندا مەیین
بێ ئەوەی فریای پەلەپیتکەی
تەقاندنی خۆیان بکەون!

بۆ ڕۆژی دوایی لەیەکە بە یەکەی کۆڵان و شەقامی
ئەم سنگە خنکاوەی مندا
لە نێو ماڵانی ئەم سییە دارزیوانەی مندا
فڕان فڕانی پەراسۆکانم بوو.
فڕان فڕانی گۆڕانییەکانم بوو.
مناڕەکان دار ئەلەکتریکی ملیان هەڵ ئەکێشام.
هەندێ دەستی خۆیشم پەنجەکانی خۆمیان ئەدزی.
سەیر بوو، ئەو ڕۆژەم قەت قەت لەبیرناچێ:

He confiscated the sticks and stones of the sky.
He became the only ruler
of this vast country of spring.
He closed the roads
between the sky and the earth.
He locked all the doors of heaven.
His voice a mixture of East and West,
he read out his first declaration.
In a space of time shorter than a leaf vibrating,
shorter than water blinking,
shorter than a lamb's bleat,
he turned the angels, cherubs, birds, and the wingless
into candles without smothering them.
He turned them into glass without breaking them.
In the coast of that silent day's black water
the flocks of doves were white
but they did not coo.
In the green fields of this dizzy day
herds of horses were lying down
but they did not neigh.

Who can stand up
before this crazy air?
Who won't get confused?
From the Zoroastrian Gathas to Marx's *Capital*,
to the swords of Zulfiqar[26]
they all threw up, blistered, then froze.
Bravery, heroism, fiery beliefs,
they all froze in their trenches
before they had time to pull the trigger.

On the next day, in every road and street
of my suffocated chest,
within the houses of these rotten lungs
my ribs were fleeing,
the songs were fleeing.
The minarets were pulling out my necks' electric poles.
Some of my hands were stealing my fingers.
It was strange! I will never forget this day:

[26] The legendary sword of Ali Ibn Abi Talib.

لە تاقە ڕاستە شەقامی ئەم لەشە ساردوسرەدا
چاوی زەقم بڕیبووە پاسدارێکی ڕیش نوورانیی
بەسەر منی هەڵەبجەوە ئەگریاو
کەچی خێرا خێرایش دەستی ئەکرد بە گیرفانیداو
لە دەنکە مێوژی گلێنەکانی سنەو سابڵاخی ئەخوارد
ئەمە حیکایەتی شانزەی مارت بوو
ئەمە هاواری خنکاوی ئەم سنگەم بوو.

‐ وەرچەرخا تاریکیم
ئەم شەوە شەوێکی جیاترە.
وەرچەرخا ڕووناکیم
ئەم خۆرە خۆرێکی جیاترە.

‐ لەم دێڕە بەولاوە
ئاوەرۆی وشەکان لە دەنگما ئەگۆڕم
لەم ڕەنگە بەولاوە
بافڵی[27] ڕەنگەکان لە چاوما ئەگۆڕم.
‐ فەرهەنگم تەنگە تەنگ، هەڵتەقی
لەبەری ئەشکەنجە و ژوار[28] دا
چوارچێوەی ئەم لەشە پابەندەم
بۆ ڕۆحی ڕافزییم دەست نادا!

‐ هەڵەبجەی "حەللاج"م چیت بینی؟!
‐ لەم بەری کەناری گیانمەوە:
بەهاری ڕموون.
گوڵی دڕ.
خۆری کوێر.
بەفری ڕەش.
"با"ی خنکاو.
ڕووباری زۆر زبر.
بارانی وشک و ڕەق.
گڕی سارد.
خوێنی زەرد.
هـــاژەی کـــەڕ.
گرمەی لاڵ. چیم بینی؟!

27 بافڵی: تاڤگە، قەڵبەزە.
28 ژوار: ئازار، ژان، ئێش.

In the only straight street of this cold body
with my popped out eyes, I was staring at a Pasdar[27]
with his glowing beard
who cried over me – Halabja,
but he regularly put hands into his pockets
and ate from the raisins of Sanandaj[28] and Mahabad's irises!
This was the story of 16th March.
This was the suffocated cry of this chest.

– My darkness turned around,
this night is a different night.
My light turned around,
this sun is a different sun.

– From this line on
I will change my voice's word-pipe.
From this colour on
I will change the waterfall of colours in my eyes.
– My dictionary is limited,
under the weight of pain and torture, it tore apart.
The frame of this imprisoned body
does not fit my heretic soul.

– Halabja, my Hallaj,[29] tell me what did you see?
– From this side of the coast of my life:
Ogre spring,
cruel flowers,
blind sun,
black snow,
suffocated wind,
rough river,
dry, hard rain,
cold flames, yellow blood,
deaf waves,
dumb explosion,
what did I see?

[27] Iranian Revolutionary Guards.
[28] Sanandaj (in Kurdish: Senendec) and Mahabad (in Kurdish: Mehabad)
are two Kurdish cities in Iran.
[29] Mansur Hallaj (in Kurdish: Hellac) was a sufi who was killed because
he was believed to be blasphemous.

کۆترى ڕق
غەدرى هەق
تاوانى فریشتە
منارەى جەردە و دز.

– ئەى لەوبەر کەنارى گیانتەوە؟
– بڵێسەى خۆڵەمێش.
شۆڕشى مردووەکان.
لافاوى وشکانیى.
هاوارى بێ دەنگیى.
پرشنگى تاریکیى.
هیواى ئائومێدیى.
سەوزایى تینوەتى.
تێرێتى برسێتى و
فڕینى کێوانم من بینى!

– لەم دێڕە بەولاوە ئاوەڕۆى وشەکان
لە دەنگما ئەگۆڕم.
لەم ڕەنگە بەولاوە بافڵى ڕەنگەکان
لە چاوما ئەگۆڕم.

* * *

هەنووکە دارسێوى شیعرێکم کۆچەریى
بنج و بێخ وەک پڕى سەرلقم بەرەڵڵا
ئەرۆم و زەویم وا لە پەڕەى دەفتەرما.
ئەرۆم و ئاسمان و باڵندەم ئەوەتان
لەسەرى بێ داڵدە و ناو جانتاى سەفەرما.

هیچ پەناوپاسار و قوژبنى چاوێکم مەگەرێن
بۆ گوڵە فرمێسکێ جێ مابێ لەو ناوە
هى خۆم و هى ئێوەیش هەمووویم.. هەر هەمووى
بە باخ و پەڕژین و جۆگەلەو.. بە درک و داڵەوە
لەگەڵ خۆم هێناوە.
من ڕەنگە لەوەختى ڕۆیشتندا ئەستێرەى شپرزەم
بزەیەک یان قاقاى شەوێکى بیرچووبێ.
من ڕەنگە لەوەختى سەفەردا شڵەژاو
گیرفانى یادێکم کون بووبێ و لەوێوە
چەند وردە خۆشیەک کەوتبنە خوارەوە.
ئەشێ من هەنارى مێ خۆشى نوکتەیەک

58

Hatred's dove,
oppressive justice,
angel's crime,
minarets of thieves and thugs.

– What about the other side of the coast of your soul?
– The flame of ashes,
the dead's revolution,
the flood of dry land,
the scream of silence,
darkness's glitter,
disappointment's hope,
the greenery of thirst,
the saturation of hunger,
the flight of mountains.

– From this line on I will change
my voice's word-pipe.
From this colour on I will change
the waterfall of colours in my eyes.

   * * *

Now I am the apple tree of a nomadic poem –
my roots are as free as my branches.
I go and my land is the pages of my book.
I go and my sky and birds
lay within my homeless head and my luggage.

Don't search the corners of my eyes
for flowers of lingering tears,
I have brought my own and yours –
all of them – with the wisteria, creeks, gardens
and thorns.
During departure, my clumsy star
may have forgotten a night smile or a laughter.
During the rush of packing
one of my memory's pockets may have leaked,
some little pleasures may have fallen out.
I may have forgotten the sweet and sour pomegranate of a joke,

یان کۆنە چاویلکەی شیعرێکم بیر چووبێ
بەڵام من ئاخر چۆن خەمتانم بیر ئەچێ!
هەتاکوو "نالی" تان لەلام بێ.
بەڵام من ئاخر چۆن ئازار و ژانتانم بیر ئەچێ
هەتاکوو "سەیوان" تان لەلام بێ.
من دەستم خۆی جادەی قیرتاوی غەمێکی درێژە..
من سەرم خۆی ئێشە گڵۆڵەی سۆزێکی ئاڵۆزە..
ئیتر چۆن خەمتانم بیر ئەچێ!

بێ کەسییم ڕووت نییە
تا ئەمرێ پۆشاکی ڕەشتانی بەش ئەکات.
تینوێتیم بێ کانی و ئاو نییە
تا ئەمرێ سیروانی چاوتانی بەش ئەکات.
تەنیاییم بێ دەنگ و کپ نییە
تا ئەمرێ هاواری ماڵتانی بەش ئەکات.
دۆزەخم بێ کزەی با نییە
تا ئەمرێ هەناسەی ساردتانی بەش ئەکات.

[...]

هەموو شەو شارەکەت سەرێکت لێئەدا
بەگوڵی ژاڵەوە شەلە شەل
خۆی ئەکا بە ژوورتا و ئەوەستێ
گوڵێکی سەر سنگیت ئەداتێو
تۆیش تاڵێوەنەوشەی ئەوینی نامۆیی ئەدەیتێ.
هەر شەوەی بەردێکی کۆڵانی دێتە لات.
هەر جارە و درەختی ماڵێکی باوەشت پیا ئەکات.
هەر شەوەی باخەڵت پڕ ئەبێلە بۆنی گەرەکێ.
ئەرۆیت و بازنەی سێبەری خەیاڵت
نانێکی سەرساجی دایکتی لەسەرە
ئەرۆیت و باوێزەی²⁹ هەناسەت
کەروێشککەی دەغڵێکی بناری وڵاتی لەگەڵە.

خۆڵی دوای بۆردومان سیماتە و ڕەنگ و ڕووت
بۆ کوێچکووی تیزماڵکی دووکەڵی گوندێکت لەگەڵە
گلێنەت "ئەزمر"ەو ئەرواریت.
دەربەندی سەگرمە و بازیان گوێچکەکەتن، گوێئەگری

---

²⁹ باوێزە: ئەو میوەیەیە کە با ئەیوەرێنێ.

or the old spectacles of a poem,
but how could I forget your sorrows
as long as your Nali is with me?
How can I forget your pain and labour
as long as your Saywan graveyard is with me?
My hand is a long pain's paved road,
my head is a tangled love's pain-hank,
so how can I forget your sorrow?

My solitude is not naked,
till death, your black garments are enough for it.
My thirst is not without spring and water
till death, the Sirwan Lake of your eyes is enough for it.
My solitude is not quiet
till death, the screams of your homes will be enough for it.
My hell is not without cold breeze
till death, your cold breaths will be enough for it.

[...]

Every night, your city visits you.
Carrying oleander blossoms, she enters your room,
limping. She stands,
gives you a flower from her chest
and you give her a lavender stalk of exile's love.
Each night, one of her road's stones comes to you.
Each time, one of her house-trees embraces you.
Each night, your embrace fills with a neighbourhood's smell.
You walk and on the circular shadow of your dreams
there is a crisp sajbread made by your mother.
You walk and your breaths' falling fruit
is accompanied with the dancing hay of your country's mountains.

The dust after bombardment is your image, colour and face.
Wherever you go the long smoke of a burnt village is with you.
Azmer mountain is your iris and you look.
The valleys of Sagrma and Bazyan are your ears, you listen.

تۆ تەنها بە بەژنی ئازاری سیروانت
قولآیی رووبار و دەریاچەو
تا زەریای جیهانیش ئەپێوێت!

[...]

هەموو جارپپالآ ئەکەوی وا هەست ئەکەیت
بووی بە تەلەبەردێلەوێبۆ جێژوان.
دائەنیشی وا هەست ئەکەیت
سەرت تۆپەلّە قورێکە لەوێ
بۆ حەمامۆکێی مناڵان
کە هەلآ ئەسیت وا هەست ئەکەیت
بووی بە پەیژەی بانیژەیەك ئیستە لەوێ.
وەختێخەوتی وا هەست ئەکەیت
بووی بە خەونی داربەرووییەك ئیستە لەوێ.

[...]

گیانی گیانم.
هەر کە بارانێئەبارێ
رائەکەم و بۆ چەند ساتێئەچمە بەری
ئەلێم بەشکوو ئەمجارەیان ئەم بارانە
بۆنی بارانی ئەزمرو گۆیژەی لێ بێ!

ئەگەر رۆژێخۆرەتاوبێ
رائەکەم و بۆ چەند ساتێئەچمە بەری
ئەو لێم ئەداو من چاو نووقاو
ئەلێم بەشکوو ئەمجارەیان ئەم هەتاوە
لە هەتاوی بەربەرۆچکەی
بن گوێسوانەی، خۆمان بچێ!

ئەگەر جار جار "با" هەلّبکات
رائەکەم و بۆ چەند ساتێئەچمە بەری
ئەلێم بەشکوو ئەمجارەیان
ئا ئەم "با"یە
وەك رەشەبای سلەیمانی
بە پرتاوبێو هەلّمبگرێو
تۆزێخۆلّ بکاتە چاوم!

لە دوورەوە هەر کە پۆلێکچم بینی
بەرەو رووییان پێهەلّئئەگرم

You can measure the depth of the rivers, lakes
and even the oceans of the world
by the height of Sirwan's pain.

[...]

Every time when you lie down
you become a stone in the lovers' meeting place.
When you sit, you imagine
that your head is a lump of clay
for the children to play with.
When you get up you turn into
a ladder to the roof of a village house over there.
When you sleep you feel that
you have become the dream of an oak tree over there.

[...]

My dearest!
Each time it rains
I run and go before it for a few seconds.
I keep thinking, maybe this time, this rainfall
will smell of the Azmer[30] and Goyja rains!

On days when the sun shines
I run and go before it for a few seconds.
The light lands on me, I close my eyes
and I keep thinking, maybe this time, this sunshine
will resemble the sun on our porch, by the walls.

If the wind blows
I run and go before it for a few seconds.
I keep thinking, maybe this time, this wind,
will be strong enough to lift me up
like the swift winds of Sulaymani,
and throw some sand into my eyes.

From afar, when I see a flock of girls
I walk faster towards them.

[30] Azmer and Goyja are mountains in Suleimanya where the poet comes from.

سەرنج ئەدەم ئەڵێم بەشکوو
نازێ، شەرمێ، تیلەی چاوێ
سوور هەڵگەڕانی گۆنایەك
بمباتەوە بۆلای شەقامی شارەکەم
وەکوو دوێنێ.

هەر کە بازاڕێکی میللیم هاتە سەر ڕێ
ڕائەکەم و ئەچمە ناوی
تیا خول ئەخۆم
ئەڵێم بەشکوو هاواری میوە فرۆشێ
هاواری ماسی فرۆشێ
هاواری سەوزە فرۆشێ
لە هاوار و ژاوەژاوی ئێواریانی مەیدانەکەو
بەر حەوزەکەو
ژێر پردەکەی خۆمان بچێ!

* * *

(کارتێکی ڕەش و سپی تایبەت بۆ هاوڕێکانم)
هاوڕێیان!
ئەم ئێوارەیە منیش دێم.
لە چایخانە بچکۆلەکە
کورسیەك بۆ شیعرم دانێن
نەیدەن بە کەس
گەر جامانە: قۆشمەکەی
"خاڵە ڕەجەب"[30] هات پێی بڵێن:
ئەبێبووری گیراوە.
گەر شەپقەکەی "ئەحەی میرزا"
بە پەلەپەل ئەویش هات بڵێن: گیراوە.
مەگەر لە هەولێرەوە میوانێك ئازیز
زۆر ماندووبێبوو بگاتە جێ
مەگەر کتێبە یاخیەکەی "عبدالخالق"[31]
وشەی شان و مل خوێناویی
کە ناتوانێ
لەبەر ئێشی زامەکانی
زۆر بەپێوە ڕابوەستێ!

[...]

[30] و ٦٠ خاڵە ڕەجەب و ئەحەی میرزا: خوا لێیان خۆشبێ، دوو پیاوی قۆشمەو قسە خۆشی خەڵکی سلێمانی بوون.
[31] عەبدولخالق مەعروف: شەهید عەبدولخالق مەعروف نووسەر و ڕووناکبیر، کە دوای هەڕەشەو هاندانی مەلاکان، ڕژێمی بەعس تیرۆریکرد.

64

I keep staring and hoping, maybe
a playful smile, a shy turning of the head,
a look from the corner of the eye, or blushing cheeks
will take me back to my city's streets, like yesterday.

Whenever I see a market
I run and go and circle around it.
I keep hoping that a fruit seller's calls,
the fish seller's calls,
the grocer's calls,
will resemble the calls and screams of the evening market
by the pond, under the bridge, back home.

    * * *

(A black and white postcard for my friends)
My dear friends!
This evening I too will join you.
Reserve a seat for my poetry
in the small teahouse,
don't give it to anyone.
If Uncle Rajab's[31] humorous Jamana[32] comes
tell him: Sorry! It is reserved.
If the hat of Ahay Mirza
comes in haste, tell him 'Sorry, it's taken'.
Except if a dear guest arrives, exhausted from Erbil –
the rebellious book of Abdul-Khaliq[33],
his battered, bleeding words,
that cannot stand on their feet for long!

    […]

[31] Both Uncle Rajab (in Kurdish: Xalle Receb) and Ahay Mirza (in
Kurdish: Eh'ey Mîrza) were known for their humour in the city of
Sulaimani.
[32] A head dress that Kurdish men wear, resembles a turban either black
and white or red and white.
[33] Abul-Khaliq Ma'aruf (in Kurdish: Abdulxalîq Me'ruf) was a writer
who was killed by the Islamic fundamentalists because of a book
he wrote.

به چواردەوری ئەڵقە ئەڵقەی بۆشاییدا
به چواردەوری خانه خانەی تەنیاییدا
چیایەکم سەر هەڵگرتوو
گوڵێکم شێت
هەر خول ئەخۆم و خول ئەخۆم.
وەڕس بوونم بۆ ساتێکیش
داڵدەی هیچ ئارامێنادا.
من دڵتەنگیم قفڵێکه خوا
چەند لێی نەوی نەیکردەوە
وەکوو "مەنسوور" زامانم جێبەخۆ ناگرن.
خانوو ویستی دابینم کات.. پەنجەرەییم لێ یاخیکرد.
شەقام ویستی دابینم کات.. شۆستەکانیم لێ یاخیکرد.
کورسی ویستی دابینم کات.. خۆمم هەڵکەن
شاران ویستیان دابینم کەن.. خەمانم باڵیان لێڕوا.

ئەی ڕۆحی وێڵ!
تەنگه به بەری عەشقی تۆ ئەم نەخشانه.
نزمه بۆ سووتانی سەرت ئەم ئاسمانه.
تەمی ئێرەت دا به خۆتا کورت و کوێر بوون.
گریان سارد و
ژانیان کپ و
پـــایزانیان بێفـــرمێسکی درشتانه.
ئەی ڕۆحی وێڵ!

ژووڕێکم هەیه تەنیاییم بەشی ناکات
تەنیاییم جمەی دێڵه دەنگ
له ڕەنگ و بۆن و تامی کۆست.
ئەو کردوێتی به نەریتێهەموو شەوێ
دووسێهاودەمی دێرینەی
وەک: هەڵەبجه
گەلی بازێ
قەڵادزێ
پیرەمەگرون

66

I am an eloping mountain,
a crazy flower.
I circle around emptiness,
around every cell of loneliness.
My loathing gives no shelter to calmness,
not even for a second.
My sadness is a lock
that even God could not unbolt.
Like Mansur[34], my wounds keep bleeding.
A house wanted to contain me
I made its window rebel against it.
A street wanted to contain me
I made its pavements rebel against it.
A chair wanted to contain me, I dug myself out.
The cities wanted to contain me,
my sorrows grew wings.

You wandering soul!
These prints are tight for the body of your love.
This new sky is low for your burning head.
You covered yourself in this place's mist
but it was too short for you.
Here, their flame is cold, their pain is quiet,
their autumns are without large drops,
you wandering soul!

I have a room that is small for my solitude.
My loneliness is brimming with sound,
with the colour, smell and taste of disaster.
My solitude has made a ritual: every night
he brings a few old friends –
like Halabja,
Geli Baze,
Qeladize[35],
Piremegrun[36],

[34] Mansur Hallaj, the sufi.
[35] Qeladize is a town which was bombarded by the Iraqi state in 1974.
Dozens of civilians were killed during the bombardment. In 1991 it was
razed to the ground. It was later rebuilt by the Kurds.
[36] A high mountain which has traces of snow through the long hot
summers, near Dukan.

لەگەڵ خۆیدا
دێنێتەوە بۆ ئەم ماڵە بچکۆلەیە
ئیتر هەتاکوو بەیانیی
تا کەلەشێری ئاوایی زامێکی تر ئەقوقێنێ
یەکە یەکە لەگەڵ بەرد و لەگەڵ دارو
لەگەڵ گەڵای هەموویاندا
سەما ئەکاو
پێئەکەنێو
ئەگری و
ئەدوێ.

ماڵێکم هەیە تەنیاییم بەشی ناکات
تەنیاییم قەرەباڵغەو پر لە ژاوەی وردە ژانە
ئەو، شەوانە بووە بە خووی
هەر لەسەر ئەم چرپا تەسکە
ئەبێلەگەڵ ڕووبارێکدا ڕابکشێو
دەست بکاتە ملی گۆمێ
چرپایش کورتە بۆ قاچەکانی ڕووبار و
تەنگیشە بۆ لەشی گەورە و پان و پۆڕی گۆمە شینێ.

ژوورێکم هەیە تەنیاییم بەشی ناکات
بۆ شپرزەییم بچووکە
تەنیاییم دۆستی بێدالدەی ئێجگار زۆرە
گەلێجاریش شەوانە وا ڕێک ئەکەوێ
تەنیاییم جێی خۆی چۆڵا ئەکاو
ژوورەکەیشی بەجێدێڵێ
تاکسپەیەکی غەریبی تازە هاتوو
لەسەر چرپای ئەو بخەوێ!

– ئەوا ئیستەیش ئەمە یەکەم پایزی دوای
کۆچی ئەسپە ڕەشی تۆیە.
ئەمە یەکەم پایزی دوای هەڵهاتنی نامۆییت و
ئاوابوونی شاخەکانی ڕۆحی تۆیە.
ئەمە یەکەم پایزی دوای
وێڵبوونی گەمیەکەی تۆیە.

لەگوێزەرەیایت.. چاوەکانت وەک کەلەپۆ.
بڕیوەتە نەهێنیی ئاو
سەرت لەناو نامۆییدا بەلەمێکی سەر گەردانەو
دەستەکانت سەوڵی شکاو.

68

to this small house
and until dawn,
till the rooster of the village crows another wound
he dances,
laughs,
cries,
talks
with each of their stones,
trees, and leaves.

I have a house that is small for my solitude.
My solitude is busy, brimming with sighing little wounds.
Every night, on this narrow bed,
he has made it a habit,
he has to lie down with a river
and to put his arms around a pond's neck
but the bed is too short for the river's legs
and too narrow for the wide, large body of the blue pond.

I have a room that is small for my solitude,
it is small for my mess.
My solitude has many defenceless friends
and many times it so happens
my solitude gives up his place
and leaves his room
so the sigh of a new exile
can sleep on his bed.

"Now this is the first autumn
after your black horse's flight.
This is the first autumn after your flight to exile,
after the mountains of your soul fell.
This is the first autumn
after your ship went astray.

You are by the ocean.
Your eyes, like the mountain where the sun sets,
are staring at the water's secrets.
Your head is a wandering boat in exile
and your hands are broken paddles.

وەکوو پایز ئێوارەی تەنیاییت تەڕە و
یادگاری لێئەچۆڕێو
خەیاڵیشت زەردەی هەتاو.

لەگوێزەریایت
شپرزەیی شەپۆلەکان و وەرینیان لە بەستێندا
پایزە مێژووی زۆر دوورن و کەفی "کات"ن و
دێن و لەگەڵا لمی عومری ئەمڕۆ و سبەی
باوەش ئەکەن بەیەکتردا
شڵپ و هووڕ حیلەی زەریایەو
داناسەکنێچەپۆکانی.
یاڵی سپی بەدەم "با"وە
هەڵ ئەپڕێو دائەڕژێو زەردوو سوورن تیسککەکانی.

لەگوێزەریایت
یەکەم جارە ئەم مێژووە شلە ببینی
یەکەم جارە ئەم سامە شینە ببینی
یەکەم جارە بۆنی تریفە بکەیت و
زڕەی ڕەنگەکان ببیسی.

لە گوێزەریایت
بەڵام لە هەڵسانەسەرپێی خێڕای ئاودا
دیسان شاخ ئەبینیتەوە
تۆ بڵێ"هەڵگورد" شیعرێکی کاکی بە کاکیت
نە گزنگت تێدا ئەڕوێو نە سۆزیشت باڵا ئەکا.

[…]

لە گوێزەریایت
گوێت لە ناڵە و گرمەگرمی سەدەکانە بەیەکدا دێن
چاوت لە زۆران گرتنی هەتاهەتای عەرد و ئاوە
چاوت لە غەزەبی خوایە کە هەڵئەچێ
چاوت لە پاشگەزبوونەوەی گوناهیشە کە دائەچێ!
چاوت لە کەفەژیلکەی غەریبیی خۆیشتە
کە کۆچ ئەکات و ون ئەبێ!

ئەمە یەکەم پایزی دوای
وێڵبوونی گەمیەکەی تۆیە
ئەم پایزە لە پایزی دایکت ناچێ

The evening of your solitude is wet, like autumn,
your memories are trickling
and your imagination is the golden sun.

You are by the ocean.
The unsettled waves lapping by the coast
are autumns of a distant history and the foam of time.
They come and with the sand of today's and tomorrow's age
they embrace each other.
The sound of waves are neighs
and their pawing does not stop.
The white mane flows in the wind
it rises and falls, its strands are yellow and red.

You are by the ocean
It is the first time you see this liquid history.
It is the first time you see this blue fear.
It is the first time you smell the moonlight
and hear the dangling colours.

You are by the ocean
but in the water's swift rising to feet
you see the mountain again.
Without Helgurd mountain you are a desert-stricken poem,
no light will grow in you,
nor will your love grow tall.

[...]

You are by the ocean.
You hear the thunder of centuries thrashing each other,
you see the eternal wrestling of water and land,
you see God's anger rise,
you see sins regress in regret,
you also see the surf of your own exile,
how it flees and disappears.

This is the first autumn
after your ship went astray.
This autumn does not resemble
your mother autumn.

ئەو پایزێکی بێوەژن، کوختەنشین، چڕ ئەوەرێ
ئەم پایزی ئاڵتوون بەسەر، تەلارنشین
لە شووشەبەندا ئەوەرێ.
ئەم پایزە لە پایزی دایکت ناچێ
لێرە هەر دار بەسەر داردا بە خوڕ ئەگریی
لێرە هەر بەرد بەسەر بەردا بەخوڕ ئەگریی
بەڵام لە پایزی دایکتا ئیستە لەوێ
داروبەردوو ئاوو خەڵکیش
هەر هەمووەیان بەیەکەوە
بەسەر خاکدا بەخوڕ ئەگرین
ئیستە لەوێ!

– لەکوێوە هاتووی؟ ئەپرسن.
دیسانەوە هەمان پرسیار ئەبێتەوە بەتوترکێوو
خوێن لە دەنگم دێنێتەوە.
وا بۆ جاری هەزار هەمین
ناوی گوڵەکەم ئەهێنم.
هەیانە وەک ڕۆژێ "با"یەک
ئەمەی دابێبە گوێیاندا
لەدوای ساتێک سەرێکی بۆ ئەلەقێنن.
بەڵام زۆریان لە بێدەنگیدا ئەخنکێن.
مت ئەبن و ملیان ئەبێبە نیشانەی سەر سوڕماندن.
منیش ئیتر لە حەژمەتا نەخشەیەکی
وەک سیاسەت چرچ و لۆچ و
پیس و دڕاو وەکوو ڕەوشتی دەوڵەتان
لە گیرفانم دەرئەهێنم.
پەنجە ئەخەمە سەر خۆری لەتوپەتم
– ئالێرەوە
لەناو کەشتیەکەی "نوح"ەوە من هاتووم و
لە بەفری "جودی"[33]دا زاوم.

– "ئێوە خەونی ڕەنگاوڕەنگی
نێو داستان و ئەفسانەی کۆنە ئەبیینن
هیواتان تراویلکەیە"[34]
منیش باوکم نیشتمانی لەناو چاویا هەڵگرتبوو
ئەو، دار خورمای بەندەرێکی
چاو خەواڵووی باکووری ئەفریقابوو
ڕۆژئێگەرداوی ئۆقیانووس ڕای فڕاندوو
لە "ئۆسلۆ"دا گیرسایەوە

---

[33] جودی: ئەو شاخەی کەشتییەکەی نوحی لەسەر گیرسایەوە وەک لە قورئاندا هاتووە.
[34] تراویلکە: سەراب.

She was a widow, cottage based, an intense fall.
This one has gold in her hair. She is castle based,
falling in a glass house.
This autumn does not resemble
your mother autumn.
Here, a tree only cries over another tree.
Here, a stone abundantly cries over another stone
but in your mother autumn, over there,
tree, stone, water and people
all together cry abundantly over homeland."

– Where do you come from? They ask me,
the same question becomes a raspberry
and makes my voice bleed.
For the thousandth time I name my flower.
Some of them nod after a second
as if a wind has once run this past their ears.
But most of them suffocate in silence,
their neck becomes an exclamation mark.
In desperation I take out a map from my pocket,
a map crumpled like politics,
torn and dirty like the ethics of nation states.
I put my finger on my divided sun.
– From here, from Noah's ship I have come!
I was born in the snow of Judi mountain.

"You are still having colourful daydreams,
daydreams in old myths and legends.
Your hope is a mirage.
My father too carried his homeland in his eyes,
he was the palm tree of a coast,
a sleepy coast in North Africa.
One day the ocean whirl chased him
and he ended up in Oslo.

له "باڕ"یّکی وەك ئێرەدا
شەوێکی سارد وەكوو ئێستا
دایكمی ناسی.
من ناوم "مارگریتا"یه
باوكم تا مرد
خەونی وەكوو خەونەكانی تۆی ئەبینیی!"

ئەمه قسەی كیژۆڵەیەكی دوورەرگی "مەغریب"ی بوو.
شەوێکی سارد، له "باڕ"یّکی سەر گەرم بووی،
ناو "ئۆسلۆ"دا وای پێوتم. میّرگیّكورو كچی
شەنگ بوون. بەدەم كەرویّشككەی گۆرانیی و مۆسیقاوه
ئەشنانەوه.
منیش هەرخۆم و شیعریّکی شەرمنۆكەم
خۆم و باڵندەی ورێنەم
خۆم و دووكەڵی جگەرەم
لەسوچیّكدا یەك یەكترمان ئەخواردەوه.

كچی دوورەرگ "مارگریتا" تازه بووه:
به "مانگ"ی ناو بەفری نەرویج
تازه بووه به هەناسەی هەڵماوی ئەم شەقامانه
به حەرفیّکی ئەم زمانەو
به پەڕی مۆسیقای ئەم "باڕ"انه.
"مەغریب" نیشتمانی باوكی
لای ئەو تەنها سیّتارماییین
سیّتارماییین و هیچی تر..
بیابانیّ، دارخورمایەك و حوشتریّ.

لەو شەوەوه "مارگریتا" ترسیّکی كرد به سیّبەرم
چركه به چركەی سەعاتیّئەم غوربەتەم ئەژمیّریّت و
بۆ كویّبرۆم تەم و مژی دیّلەگەڵم.
لەو بارەوه مارگریتا گومانیّکی تیا رۆكردم
وەكوو خۆرکه لەو ساكەوه
پەلكەكای خەونم ئەخواو
لەناو بیّشەی تاریكیدا
نائومیّدیی دائەتاشیّبۆ تابووتی
مانگەشەوم.

لەوشەوەوه وا هەست ئەكەم سیمای كچه بچكۆلەكەم
لەبەرچاوم بۆته سیمای مارگریتا
نیگاكانی چوونەته ناو نیگایەوه
جۆگەی دەنگی رژاوەته ناو دەنگیەوه

74

One cold night, in a bar like this one
he met my mother.
My name is Margarita.
Till he died, my father
had similar dreams to yours."

These were the words of a half Moroccan girl.
She told me this on a cold night,
in a busy bar in Oslo. They were a grove of
cheerful girls and boys. They swayed
to the rabbiting of music and songs.
I was sitting with a shy poem –
the bird of my hallucination and myself,
the smoke of my cigarettes and myself
were eating each other up in a corner.

The mixed girl, Margarita, has become
the moon in the snow of Norway.
She has become the steamy breath of these streets,
a letter in this language,
the wings of music in these bars.
Morocco, her father's country,
is only three images in her mind,
three phantoms and nothing else:
a desert, a date-tree and a camel.

From that night on, Margarita turned fear into my shadow,
the kind of fear which counts every second of my exile
and brings its fog wherever I go.
From that bar on, Margarita planted doubt in me,
one which is consuming my dreams,
carving out disappointment for my nights' coffin
in the cradle of darkness.

From that night on my youngest daughter's face
has become that of Margarita's,
her vision has penetrated my daughter's,
her voice has spilt into her voice,

باخی قژیان هەر یەك باخەو
رەنگەكانی هەست و نەستیان بوون بە یەك رەنگ.
لەو شەوەوە وا هەست ئەكەم
منیش كچە بچكۆڵەكەم
نامۆیی گەورەی كردووە
وەكوو دڵۆپە شەوەنمێ
تێكەڵا بە "با"ی ئێرە بووە
لەسەماگەی نیوەشەودا
سەری لە لەشی ونبووەو
جاربەجارئیلە بارێكدا بۆی ئەگەرێ.
وا هەست ئەكەم هەموو رۆژێ
تارماییەك دێت بۆلام و وێنەیەكیم بۆ ئەكێشێ:
كاڵبوونەوەی یادگاری.
رووتانەوەی پەروباڵی زمانەكەی.
هەڵورینی خێزانەكەی.
بیرچوونەوەی خەونی باوكی.
بۆن نەكردنی هەناسەی نیشتمانی.
توانەوەی بەفری گۆرانی و
حیكایەتی گیانی دایكی.

لەو شەوەوە وا هەست ئەكەم
منیش باوكی مارگریتام
بووم بە شیعری خەمێكی زەرد
رۆژێلە بەفری مەنفادا ئاوا دەبم!.
ئەوسا لەوەرزێكی تردا
شەوێكی سارد وەكوو ئێستا لەبارێكدا
ئەویش وەكوو مارگریتا
باسم ئەكا:
"باوكم مەڵێكی كێویی بوو
لە شاخەوە باڵی گرت و
گەیشتە بەفری ئەم قوتبەو
رۆژێلێرە، بەدەم ئاواز خوێندنەوە
خەونەكانی لەگەڵ خۆیدا رەق بوونەوە!"

* * *

مێژووم و سەفەر ئەكەم و
لەگەڵ خۆمدا شۆرشەكانم ئەگێرم
لەخۆم زیاتر كەس تەماشای خوێنم ناكات.

76

the garden of their hair is the same
and the colours of their emotions have become one.
From that night on I feel
my young daughter
has also been raised by exile
and like a drop of dew
she's mixed with the wind of this place.
Her body has lost her head
on the night's dance floor
and every now and then she looks for it in a bar.
I feel that every day
a phantom comes and draws her picture for me:
The fading of her memories,
the moulting of her language,
the fall of her family,
forgetting her father's dream,
being unable to smell the breath of homeland,
the melting of songs' snow
and her mother's stories.

From that night on I feel
that I too father Margarita.
I have turned into a yellow sorrow's poem
and one day I will set in the snow of exile.
Then, in another season,
in a cold night like this one, in a bar,
my daughter too will talk about me
like Margarita:
(My father was a mountain bird.
He flew the mountain
and reached the snow of this pole.
One day here, as he was singing
his dreams froze with him!)

        * * *

I am history in motion,
I tour my revolutions with me,
no one but myself looks at my blood.

دووکەڵم ئەسووڕێمەوە
لەگەڵ خۆمدا دێهاتەکانم ئەگێڕم
لەخۆم زیاتر چاوی کەس ناکزێتەوە
بەم دووکەڵە.
لاواندنەوەم ئەخولێنمەوە و لەگەڵ خۆمدا
سێدارەکانم ئەگێڕم
لەخۆم زیاتر کەس گوێناگرێلەم کۆتەڵە
چیرۆکم دڕێژ ئەمەوەو
لەگەڵ خۆمدا قرچەقرچی شەقامەکانم ئەگێڕم
لەخۆم زیاتر کەس بۆنی بۆکرووز ناکات
لەخۆم زیاتر لە خۆم
لەخۆم زیاتر
لەخۆم..

کوا غوربەت سێبەری داربەڕووی دوورییە؟
گەر وایە! ئەم هەموو کڵاوی فرمێسکی بەڕوانە
چی ئەکەن لەلای من؟ بۆ لێرەن؟
بۆ ڕیزیان بۆ سەری قەڵەلەمم گرتووە؟
کوا غوربەت ئەستێرەی پەمەیی کۆچ کردووو
سیوەیلە و نەیبینم؟ کوا وایە؟
گەر وایە؟ ئەم هەموو وەنەوشەی خەونانەی
"زێ" و "نۆڕک"[35]
چین لە ناو دەفتەرما ڕواون؟
بۆ لێرەن؟
بۆ ژووری تەماشام پڕئەکەن
لەبۆنی دوو "بارێ"ی پاش باران؟

کوا غوربەت شەوقە بۆ ئاژاوەی ئێوارەی
منداڵی گەڕەك و نەیبیستم؟ کوا وایە؟
گەر وایە؟ منداڵی ئەم هەموو گەڕەکە
لەکووچەی ناو دەنگما چی ئەکەن؟!
بۆ لێرەن؟
بۆ ساحەی فتبۆڵیان سەرسنگمەو
گاڵتەیان: تریقەی کاغەزی سپیم و
شەڕیشیان: "مسوەدە"م؟
کوا غوربەت بای بۆنی شارێکە من نەیکەم؟
کوا وایە؟ گەر وایە؟
ئەم بۆنە تێکەڵەی: ڕاڕەوی قەیسەری و
مەیدانی ماستەکە و، گوزەری زین درووو..

---

[35] زێ و نۆڕك و هەردوو بارێ: چەند گوندێکی بناری سوورکێوی ناوچەی (سیوەیل) بوون رژێمی عێراق وێرانی کردن.

I am smoke and I wander,
I tour my villages with me,
my smoke burns no one's eyes but my own.
I am lamentations and I circle,
I tour my gallows with me,
no one but myself listens to this Kotel.
I am a story extending
and I tour the blazing of my roads with me,
no one smells the burning but myself,
no one but me
no one but
no one
no.

Who says exile is distance's oak-tree shadow?
If it is, what are all these acorn-caps
doing by me? Why are they here?
Why have they queued to cap my pen?
Who says exile is Siweil's[37] fled stars
that I can't see? How is it like that?
If it is, then what are all these lavender dreams
of Ze[38] and Norik doing in my book? Why are they here?
Why do they fill my vision's room
with the smell of the two Barehs[39] after rain?

Who says exile is longing for
the neighbourhood children's chaos in the evening?
If it is, then what are all the neighbourhoods' children
doing in the roads of my voice? Why are they here?
Why is my chest their football field,
their jokes my laughing white pages
and their fights my rough drafts?
Who says exile is the smell of an absent city?
How is it like that? If that is true
then how is it possible for the smell of the bazaar,
the yoghurt square and the saddle maker's passage

[37] The star of Siweil (in Kurdish: Sîweyl) is famous for only appearing at certain times of the year.
[38] Ze and Norik are villages in Siweil.
[39] Little Bareh and Big Bareh are two beautiful villages in the Siweil region.

چین که دێن له حێلی وشەم و
له پوونگەی کاکۆڵم و
له چەرمی جانتاکەم؟!

ئەی تەنیایی!
ئەی ئەسپی ڕەشی بێزاربوو
لەجڵەوی ئەم زەمانی بازرەبوونە![37]
ئەی زایەڵەی کەوە سوورەکەی ناو سنگم
تۆ کەی ئەوەندە چواردەوری
جێژوانی ڕازەکانت چۆڵا و هۆڵا بوون؟
لەناو لانکەی نیشتماندا
تۆ هاوڕێی ئەمەکداری لاواندنەوەت
گەلێزۆڕ بوون.
تۆ کوا لەوێهەرگیز هەستت
به بزربوونی جریوەی بێداریت و
خاوبوونەوەی ژێی گینگڵی شەوان ئەکرد؟
تۆ کوا لەوێهەرگیز هەستت
به ونبوونی جێپێی ئاخ و
ساردبوونەوەی ئاگردانی گریان ئەکرد؟
تۆ کوا لەوێقەت هەناسەت
بێدەربەندی هاودەم بووە؟
تۆ لەوێخەمە دراوسێت هێندە هەبوون
به پەیژەی وەخت و ناوەختا
دڵسۆزیتان، سمۆرە بوون
بۆلای یەکتر دائەبەزین.. سەر ئەکەوتن.
بەسەر دیواری مابێندا فرمێسکەکان بازیان ئەداو
وەکوو لاولاوی سەر دەرگاو پەنجەرەتان
ماچ ئەرۆیشت و ماچ ئەخشاو
لەسەربان و له حەوشەدا، وەک تەنافی جلەکانتان
ڕازو نیازتان تێکەڵا ئەبوون.

ئەی تەنیاییم!
تۆ لێرە ئیستە کەناریی
ناو ژانێکی شووشەبەندی ڕەنگاوڕەنگی
بەم دەنووک بەوباڵانه
چۆن ئەتوانی تۆ سنووری شووشه ببڕی؟
بۆ کوێئەفڕی
ئەی تەنیایی؟!

[37] بازرە بوون: ئاوارەبوون.

to rise from the cardamom of my words,
the pennyroyal of my forelock
and the leather of my bag?

Loneliness!
You black horse, fed up with exile's rein!
You, echo of the singing partridge in my chest!
When has your secrets' land been so empty?
In the cradle of homeland
you had many loyal friends for lament.
When did you ever notice the loss
of your insomnia's birdsong,
the slowing down of the cords of your agitation?
When did you ever feel the loss
of a sigh's footsteps
and the cooling of the crying hearth, over there?
When was your breath ever
without a valley of companions?
You had many neighbouring sorrows over there.
Your loyalties were squirrels,
they climbed up and down the ladder of good and bad times.
Your tears jumped over your parting wall.
Like the ivy on your doors and windows
kisses were sent, kisses would slide.
In your courtyards, on your rooftops,
your secrets and wishes mingled with each other
like your wash lines.

Loneliness!
Now you are a canary trapped in pain, colourful and glazed.
How can you break the glass
with your beak and your wings?
Where will you fly to,
loneliness?

جیابوونەوەی ئەم باڵانە لەو ئاسمانە
لەنگەری گیانیان تێکداوم.
دوورکەوتنەوەی ئەم وشانە لەو گوڵانە
هەستی بۆنکردنی خاکیان تیا وەراندووم.
دوورکەوتنەوەی ئەم چاوانە لەو کێوانە
زنەی سەرنجیان کزکردووم.
جیابوونەوەی ئەم دەستانە لەو پرچانە
پەنجەی تەماسیان سڕکردووم.
دوورکەوتنەوەی ئەم زمانە لەو تامانە
ئۆخەی چێژیان لەناو دەمدا بزرکردووم.
جیابوونەوەی ئەم قاچانە لەو ڕێیانە
ناونیشانی زۆر هەواریان تیا ونکردووم.
جیابوونەوەی ئەم گوێیانە لەو بەستانە
چەند هاژەیان تیا کەرکردووم.
ــ نامۆیی چییە؟ لێی پرسیم.
وەکوو فیشکەی شەمەندەفەری هەزارپێ
شەو دریژ و ئاخ دریژ و دووکەڵی یادم دریژبوو.
شەوقی گڵۆپی زەردباوی کابینەکە
ئەیدا لە تەمی دەروونم
لەو ساتەدا وام هەست ئەکرد:
من دەشتێکی چۆڵا و هۆڵی
وەکوو ئەو دیو پەنجەرەکەم!.
وەك جانتاکەم شەوگار هەر تەکەتەکی بوو
خەوی زڕاو بووبوو بە جامێکی مس و
لەگەڵا هەموو سەرسمێکی ئەو شەوەدا
لەسەرما ئەزرنگایەوە.
لەو ساتەدا وام هەست ئەکرد:
گڵۆپی زەردباو هەر خۆمم
تەم هەر خۆمم
هێڵی ئاسنیش هەر خۆمم
ڕێگا خۆمم و کۆچ هەر خۆمم.

– نامۆیی چییە؟ لێی پرسیم.
مەی: ئەستێرکێکی کڵپەبوو
سەرم تیا نوقم کردبوو.
خەیاڵی لەرزۆك لانکەم و
بێهودەیی ڕای ئەژەنیم.

The separation of these wings from that sky
destroyed the balance of my soul.
The separation of these words from those flowers
wilted my sense of smell.
The separation of these eyes from those mountains
weakened the spring of my vision.
The separation of these hands from those plaits
numbed my fingers and my touch.
The separation of this tongue from those flavours
made me lose the pleasure of taste.
The separation of these legs from those paths
made me lose the address of many loved places.
The separation of these ears from those songs
deafened many echoes in me.
– What is exile? She asked me.
Like the whistle of the centipede train
the night was long, my sigh was long
and the smoke of my memory was long.
The yellow light in the cabin
shone on the fog of my soul.
In that moment I felt:
I was a bare field, like the one behind the window.
The night kept trembling, like my luggage.
My lost sleep was like a copper bowl,
echoing in my head
with every stumble of the night.
In that moment I felt:
I was the yellow light,
I was the fog,
I was the railway tracks,
and the roads and the journey were me.

– What is exile? She asked me.
Wine was a pond of flame
I had drowned my head in it.
The unstable imagination was my cradle
and purposelessness was rocking me.

لەو ساتەدا وام هەست ئەکرد:
شووشەیەک مەیی ڕژاوم
شووشەیەک بادەی شکاوم و
هەر بە تەنها ملەکەمم پێوە ماوەو
ئەم جیهانەیش تووری داوم!

– نامۆیی چییە؟ لێی پرسیم. چی پێبلێم؟
بلێم: دڵداریی نێوانی خەون و خاکە؟
یان هەناسەی گوڵێکە دوور لە باخی خۆی؟
یان وێڵبوونی تەماشایە بەدوای یادەکانی خۆیدا؟!
یان تەنیاییە ئەو کاتەی ڕەوئەکات و
نیشتمانی لەکۆڵدایە؟!
یان ئاوێنەیە و بۆ سیمای یادێئەگریی؟
چی پێ بلێم؟! بلێم: نانێکی سەرساجە و بیری ئەکەم؟
بلێم: بۆنی مێخەک بەندەو بۆنی دایکم و
بۆنی کچانی گەڕەکەو ئیستە نایەن؟

بلێم: شێتبوونی ڕێواسە
دوور لە کەلیخانی وڵات؟
بلێم: مەراقی سووری هەناری ئاوارەیە
بۆ شارەبان؟!
یان سەودای زەردو سپییە بۆ نێرگز و
یان شەیدا بوونێکی سەوزە بۆ بەهاران؟!
بلێم: دووریی نێوان من و کورسیەکە
لەچایخانە بچکۆڵەکە؟!
نێوان من و مێزی یانە و ئێوارانی چیمەنەکە؟!
چی پێبلێم؟ بلێم: نامۆیی، دیوارە؟
یان بلێم عیشقە بۆ قوڕی کۆڵانان و
بینینەوەی شێتەکانی شارەکەم و
یان ماچێکی باڵکراوەو ناگاتەوە ئەو هەوارە؟!
من لە دوایدا پێی ئەلێم:
شپرزەیی هێندە باڵی نامۆییمی ڕاکێشاوە
تۆری گلێنەم ڕایەڵی تیشکەکانی
خاوبۆتەوەو
لەم دوورەوە وەختێئەڕوانمە نیشتمان:
هەموو یادێ، هەموو شوێنێ

84

In that moment I felt:
I was a spilt glass of wine,
a broken bottle of alcohol,
I only had my bottle neck left
and the world had thrown me away.

– What is exile? She asked me. What shall I tell you?
Shall I say: it is the love between land and dreams?
Or the sigh of a flower, away from her own garden?
Or the wandering of a vision, looking for its memories?
Or loneliness when she flees
and carries her country on her shoulders?
Or it is a mirror that looks for a memory's image?
What shall I say? Shall I say: it is a nan-bread on the saj-tray
and I miss it?
Shall I say it is the lost smell of a string of cloves,
the smell of my mother,
the smell of the neighbourhood girls that has forsaken me?

Shall I say it is the rhubarb going crazy
away from the Keli Khan[40] of homeland?
Shall I say it is the exiled pomegranates' red longing
for Shareban[41]?
Or the fervour of yellow and white for narcissus?
Or a green passion for the spring?
Shall I say it is the distance between me and a chair
in the little tea-house back home?
Between me and the bar's table
and the warm evenings on the grass?
What shall I tell you? Shall I say exile is a wall?
Or shall I say it is love for the mud roads,
for seeing the mad people of my city
and a wing-clipped kiss which will not reach home?
At the end I tell her:
Distress has stretched the wings of my exile,
the threads of my irises have lost focus.
From this distance when I look at my homeland:
every memory, every place,

---

[40] Keli Khan (in Kurdish: Kelîxan) is a region famous for its rhubarb.
[41] The pomegranates of Shareban (in Kurdish: Şareban) are famous.

هەموو خەونێ، لەبەرچاوی یادگارم
ئەبن بە دووان، ئەبن بە سیان
ئەبن بە دە.. ئەبن...
چی پێبلێم؟!
چی پێبلێم؟!
چی؟!

[...]

هەر ئەمشەو درەنگان لە کەنار
ئەو گۆمە غەمگینەی تەنیشتمان
ئەو کاتەی مانگ سەری ورِی خۆی
ئەخاتە سەر شانی گردۆڵکەو
"با"یش ئەروا بۆ سەمای هێواشی
هاوینەی لێرەوار.
هەر ئەمشەو ئەوکاتەی کە لمی
لەش گەرمی بەستێنیش وەکوو بەرد
شەکەتە و خەواڵوو.
ئەو ساتەی گژوگیا
بەرامبەر تریفەی حەپەساو
بەوەنەوز پێڵویان قورس ئەبێو
کەنەفت و ملیان لار!

هەر ئەمشەو ئەوکاتەی فریشتەی داستان و
پەریەکان، لە پەردەی زیوینی کەژاوەی ئاوەوە
رووت و قووت دێنەدەر، ئەلڵقاوئەلڵق دەس ئەگرن
بەچرپە ئەدوێن و چراوگی ئەوینیان
ئەخەنە سەر زینی شەپۆل و
(تانجیك)ی نوور ئەدەن
لەقژی درێژیان.

هەر ئەمشەو رِێیەکی شین باوی نەهێنیی
ئەمباتە کەناری ئەو گۆمەی تەنیشتمان
لەشوێنێك نەپندی
نەپندی[38] وەك جێگژوانی بەفری خواو
بڵێسەی عەشقێکی ئەبەدیی
چەپەك وەك، ژێر کەپرە ساردەکەی
دەروونی غەریبان
کرِ وەکوو سێبەری تەنیایی
شەوانی غەریبان.

_____
[38] نەپندی: نەهێنیی، نا ئاشکرا، شاراوە.

every dream before the eyes of my memory
become two, become three
become ten… become…
What shall I tell you?
What shall I tell you?
What?

[…]

Later tonight by the shore
of the sad pond beside us,
when the moon lays its giddy head
on the hill's shoulder
and the wind goes to the woods' slow summer dance;
just this night when the shore's warm sand
is as tired and sleepy as the stone;
when standing before the stunned moonlight
the eyelids of the bushes droop
and their necks bend;

just this night when from the water's silver curtains
the stories' angels and fairies come out all naked,
hold hands in a circle, speak in whispers,
place their love's flare on the waves' saddle,
crown their long hair with light;

just this night, a secret blue path
will take me to the shore of the pond beside us
to a secret place, secret like the meeting
of God's snow with an eternal love's flames;
a remote place, like the cold hut of displaced souls,
quiet like the shadow of loneliness in exile's nights.

وەکوو عەشق
سۆز ئەمبا
رەنگە لای برینی بێناڵەی دارمێوێ
لابداو دامبنێ.
رەنگە لای سووتانی بێدەنگی دار بییەك.
رەنگە لای هەناوی کۆڵراوی گا بەردێ.

چەند ساڵە من لێرە بنچکی
سەر ژیلەی، چاوەڕێی ئەمشەوەم
چەند ساڵە من سەرم هەوورێکی نەبارەو
چاوەڕێی هاتنی بارانی ئەم خەوەم.
من ئەمشەو:
مەچەکم و چاوەڕێی پەنجەمم.
قاچم و چاوەڕێی رێگەمم.
پژوپۆم سەرکۆنەی "با"ی زۆرکرد
بۆ نەهات؟ تافگەی ئەو زەڵمە بۆ نەهات؟
نەگەیشت، ئەو هاژەی ئەوینە، نەگەیشت.
باڵندەی پرسیارم بە دەنووك
کراسە شینەکەی سامالیان کونکون کرد
بۆ نەهات؟ ئەو کۆتری هەتاوە.. بۆ نەهات؟
نەگەیشت؟ ئەو خەمە سەرکەشەم، نەگەیشت؟
بۆ نەهات؟ ئەو رەزی هۆنراوە سپیانە، بۆ نەهات؟

ئەو کە هات دڵنیام
لەگەڵ خۆی نیشتمان ئەهێنێ
لە قولی مشتیدا کێوان و لەپێڵوی ماندوویدا
دەریاچە ئەهێنێ.
ئەو کە هات دڵنیام
ئەوینی شارەزوور تەرتەری کردووە.
ئەو ئیستە سۆزێکە شەڵاڵی غوربەتەو
بە باڵی چریکە لەسەر تەم ئەنووسێو
تەرزەیەو
شەختەیەو
ئاگری گرتووە!
ئەو کە هات دڵنیام
هەر یەکسەر هەواڵی
دارچوالەی ئاوارەی "زەردیاوا"[39] ئەپرسێ!
پەرۆشە
پەرۆشە

---

[39] زەردیاوا: ناوی دێرینەی قەرەداغ.

Affection, like love, takes me:
It may stop
and drop me off by the silent wound of a vine,
next to the silent burning of a willow
or by the carved soul of a boulder.

For many years I was twigs on embers,
waiting for this night.
For many years my head was a barren cloud
waiting for this dream to rain.
Tonight, I am a wrist waiting for my fingers,
a pair of feet waiting for my path,
a mouth waiting for my speech.
My branches reproach the wind many times:
Why didn't he come? Why didn't Zellm's cascade come?
He didn't arrive... that splashing wave of love didn't arrive.
The birds of my questions pecked
and pierced the blue sky with their beaks:
Why didn't he come? That dove of sunlight... why didn't he come?
He didn't arrive, my rebellious sorrow, why didn't he arrive?
Why didn't he come? That vineyard of white poems, why
    didn't he come?

I am certain that when he comes
he will bring homeland with him –
in his fist he will bring the mountains,
in his tired eyelids,
the lakes.
When he arrives
I am certain he is soaked in Sharezur's love.
Now he is affection drenched in exile,
he writes on the fog with his song's wings
he is hailstone,
he is frost,
blazing!
I am certain as soon as he comes he will ask
about the almond trees exiled from Zerdyawa.
He is fervent
fervent

بۆ ئەوەی گەڵایەك فرمێسکی
دارەکەی "شێخ هەباس" ببینێ
سووتاوە بۆ ئەوەی، ڕێحانە بسکێکی
کچێکی سنەیی بۆن بکاو
شێت بووە بۆ ئەوەی
لە دەشتی بەرینی دەنگێکدا
هۆرەیەك ببیسێ.

[…]

نازانم پێشوازیی عاشقێلە خۆری عاشقان چۆن ئەکرێ؟
نازانم پێشوازیی غەریبێلە مانگی غەریبان چۆن ئەکرێ؟
نازانم ئەو وەختەی گەڵایەك
ئەگاتە بەردەمی زریانێچی ئەڵێ؟
یان تاقە دڵۆپێلە ئەوین
ئەو وەختەی ئەگاتە
زەریایەك لە ئەوین.. چی ئەڵێ؟!

[…]

من کە چووم بە نیازم لەگەڵا خۆم لەسنگما
ڕۆژنامەی: ڕەشەبای خوێناویی دوو سەدەی
کێوانی بۆ بەرم.
یادداشتی: دووکەڵی زامانی دوو سەدەی
پێدەشت و بناری بۆ بەرم.
بەنیازم ئەڵبووومی: ڕەنگینی ئازاروژان و سوێی
قرچان و سووتان و زریکەی
ئاو، گڵ، دار، بەرد، شار، گوند
ئاژەڵا و باڵدار و بێباڵی
دوو سەدەی بۆ بەرم!
بەنیازم وەختێچووم لەگەڵا خۆم لە چاوما
بەتایبەت
ئاسمانی خنکاوی "هەڵەبجە"ی بۆ بەرم.

[…]

بەڵێنە هەر ئەمشەو درنگان دوو قۆڵیی
لە کەنار ئەو گۆمە غەمگینەی تەنیشتمان:
من و مەلا خدری ئەحمەدی شاوەیسیی مکایڵی پێکبگەین:
پێکبگەین وەکوو دوو پەپوولە
پایزەی گیرساوەی سەر درکێ!
وەکوو دوو بریسکەی کشانی ئەستێرەی ناو خەونێ.

to see the leaf-tear
of the Shekh Hebas tree.
He is burning to smell the basil hair-strands
of a girl from Sanandaj.
He is passionate
to hear a folksong
in the open field of a voice.

[...]

I don't know how a lover welcomes love's sun?
I don't know how an exile welcomes exile's moon?
I don't know what a leaf says
when it reaches a storm?
When a drop of affection
reaches the ocean of love, what does it say?

[...]

In my chest I plan to take the newspaper
of two centuries of the mountain's bloody wind for him.
I will take the memoranda of two centuries
of smoke from the fields' and valleys' wounds.
I intend to take the colourful album of two centuries of pain,
the labour and disappointment of the blazing and screaming
water, clay, tree, stone, city, village
animal, birds and the wingless.
I will especially take
the suffocated sky of Halabja,
in my eyes.

[...]

It is planned that later tonight
by the shore of the sad pond beside us
Mullah Khidir Ahmed Shaways Michaeli[42] and I meet,
like two dandelions resting on a thorn,
like the glitters of a star falling in a dream,

---

[42] Nali's full name (in Kurdish: Malla Xidir Ehmed Şawaysî Mîkayalîl).

وەکوو دوو زەمانی ئاوێتەی یەك کۆچ و ڕەوەندێ.
وەکوو دوو قەسیدەی گریاوی یەك دیدە.
وەکوو دوو باڵندەی غەریبیی ئاسمانێ.

بەڵام من ئەزانم ئەو زێیەی
لەگیانی بێئۆقرەی شیعرمدا بۆی ئەبەم
هەناسەی سوورترە،
زریکەی بەخوڕتر،
فرمێسکی درێژترە،
لەشێوە سوورەکەی سنگی ئەو.
بەڵام من ئەزانم ئەو بێشەی ژوارەی
کە ئەیدەم بە کۆڵی سەیوانا و بۆی ئەبەم
هەنسکی چڕترە
سێبەری وەیشوومەی کرترو
قوڵپەکەی بەربینی درەختی پڕترە
لەسارای خاك و خۆڵا.
بەڵام بۆ شیعری جوان، زرنگەی پاوانە
قەسیدەی شۆخ و شەنگ
بۆ کانە پرشنگی هزری ورد، بارانی خەیاڵا و
بریقەی هەستی تەڕ
پێی ئەڵێم:
بێگومان.. سەروەرەم!.. بێگومان
وشەی تۆ قوڵترە
حەرفی تۆ گەشترە
دەنگی تۆ پڕترە.. بێدەعوام، پەتکیش نیم!

[...]

هەر ئەم شەو درەنگان دوو قۆڵیی
لە کەنار ئەو گۆمە غەمگینەی تەنیشتمان
یەکتریی ئەبینین
جڤینی غەریبان ئەم شەوە
سووتانی غەریبان ئەم شەوە
ئەو وەختەی ئەگاتە بەردەممم
ئەو ئاوە و من داربی و کرنووشی بۆ ئەبەم.
ئەیبینم: چڵێکی دارەکەی "پیرمەسوور"
گۆچانی دەسێتی.
ئەیبینم: ڕێئەکا و دوو سێپۆڵ چۆلەکەی "کانی با"
بەدەوری دەغڵەکەی ئەو سەروڕیشەدا خول ئەخۆن.
ئەیبینم دووراو دوور ئەیبینم!

like two time zones overlapping in exile,
like two crying poems of one vision,
like two birds of one sky of exile.

But I know that the ocean which I will take for him
in the restless body of my poems,
has redder breaths,
more fluent screams,
longer streams of tears,
than the red river of his chest.
But I know the grove of pain I take to him
on the back of Seywan graveyard
has more crowded cries.
The shadow of its distress is quieter,
the simmering of its trees fuller
than the desert of Khakukhol.[43]
As for beautiful poems, the jingling anklets
of elegant long verse,
the light-mine of deep thoughts, the rain of imagination,
the glittering of wet emotions, I will tell him:
No doubt… my lord! No doubt!
Your words are deeper,
your letters more vibrant,
your voice is fuller… I will not argue.

[…]

Later this night
by the shore of the sad pond beside us
the two of us will meet.
Tonight is the gathering of exiles.
Tonight is the blazing of exiles.
When he reaches me
he is water and I am the willow tree and I bow to him.
I see him: a branch of the Pirmesur tree
is his walking stick.
I see him: he walks and flocks of sparrows from Kani Ba
are circling the crops of his hair and beard.

---

[43] Khakukhol (in Kurdish: Xakûxol) is the village where Nali was born.

پەلەیەك گوڵجاری گوندەکەی "ماڵیاوا"
سەرپێچی سەرێتی.

[...]

ئەوەندەم پێ ئەکرێهەر کە هات
تریفەی بۆ بکەم بە فەرش و
لەبەر پێی سیروانیا ڕای بخەم.
ئەوەندەم پێئەکرێ
لە دوودی هەناسەی درەختی عەلەم دار
وەك لاکێش
پارچەیەك لە دووکەڵا ببڕم و ئەستێرەی
ئەم دڵەی پێوەکەم بۆ ئەوەی بۆی بکەم
بە ئاڵای پێشوازیی ورشەدار.

[...]

پێی ئەڵێم:
گەورەم تۆ!
لەدوای خۆت بۆ ئێمە
میراتی خەمێکت بەجێهێشت
بەردەوام بە هاژە و کەف چڕین وەك زەڵم و
کەڵگەت وەك هێرۆی قژ سووری
گوێزامی تانجەرۆ!

بەڵێنە هەر ئەم شەو درەنگان لە کەنار
ئەو گۆمە غەمگینەی تەنیشتمان دوو قۆڵیی
یەکتری ببینین!
هەر ئەم شەو، من، نالی، حەزرەتی غەریبان ئەبینم.
ئەو، شەوە لە گزنگ موتوربە کراوە ئەبینم.
ئەو، کێوە کۆچەرە ئەبینم.
ئەو، بەفرە فەرەنجی لەبەرە ئەبینم.
هاوینە و لەماڵی پایزدا جڤینی غەریبانە ئەم شەوە.
لە کوێوە داربەڕووی لانەواز
ڕەگ ئەدا بە کۆڵیا و ئەگاتە ئەم ناوە؟
لەکوێیە پرشنگی دەربەدەر؟
لەکوێیە ڕووباری ئاوارە؟

I see him, from afar I see him:
a garden of flowers from Malyawa[44] village
adorns his turban.

[…]

When he comes I can only
make the moonlight his carpet
and unroll it before Sirwan lake's feet.
I can only cut out a rectangular piece of smoke
from the breaths of Alamdar's[45] tree-like figure
and hang the star of this heart on it
to make him a glistening welcome flag.

[…]

I will tell him:
My lord!
After you left
we inherited your sorrow,
a sorrow which roars forever like Zellm,
it is tall as the ginger marshmallow,
by the wound of Tanjero river!

It is planned that later tonight
by the shore of the sad pond nearby
the two us meet!
Just this night, I will meet Nali, the king of exiles.
I will meet that night which is grafted with sunrise,
I will meet that migrating mountain.
That Ferenji[46] – wearing snow.
It is summer and in the house of autumn
the gathering of exiles is tonight.
How will the homeless oak tree
de-root itself and arrive here?
Where is the destitute sun-ray?
Where is the exiled river?

[44] Malyaway is the village where Nali's beloved, Habiba, came from.
[45] Marif Alamdar (in Kurdish: Marif Elemdar) was a writer.
[46] Traditional Kurdish coat made of sheep skin.

ئەستەمبوولا، لانکەیە بۆ هەتاو؟
ئیستگەیە بۆ خەونی غەریبان؟
یان تۆڕە بۆ مانگ و چەقۆیە بۆ ملی ئەستێران؟
ئەستەمبوولا دەروازەی بارانە؟
یان شاری کوللەیە و شمشێری دەس سولتان؟
ئەستەمبوولا سروەیە؟! ئارامە؟! هەتوانە؟!
یان خوێیە بۆ زامی گەریدەی عاشقان؟!
لەوێوە نالیی دێو شارەزوور لەگەڵ خۆی ئەهێنێ.

[...]

کە گەیشت پێی ئەڵێم: سەروەرم!
سەرکردەی لەشکری خەم و داخ!
مەترسە لە دوای تۆیش سوپاکەی خەمامان
بەهێزە و سەرکەوتوو،
لەدوای تۆیش نەشکاوین، بۆ بشکێین؟!
کەشادیی ئەوەندە لاوازبێو ترسنۆک
بۆ بشکێین؟!
کە خۆشیی هێندە زوو
لەبەردەم هێرشی کۆستماندا ببەزێ!

[...]

من ئیستاکە وشەم لەناو دەفری شیعرا ئەگرمەوە،
خەون و سروشت و رەنگ و دەنگ تێکەڵا ئەکەم.
وێنەی "نالیی" وا ئەکێشم:
سیمایەکی: بەزەرکەفتی ئەشکەنجەو داخ درەوشاوە
یان گردە تەمێکی تێکەڵا بە زەردەپەری ئێواران.
دوو چاوی روون، لە بنیاندا چەوی خەیاڵا تروسکەی دێ.
دوو گۆی ورشەدارن لەناو دوو کاڵانەی قوڵا و ماتدا
بزاڤیان تیژ و بێئۆقرە.
بە سەریانەوە دوو بروّی تەنک، پەیوەست
بەردە نوێژی تەوێڵێکیان هەڵگرتووە
کە باران و گوڵا و شیعر
نوێژی لەسەر دائەبەستن.
دوو روومەتی پڕ لە دێراو
بە "جووت"ی ساڵ رێزرێبوون و
کەوتوونە بەرچریی سێبەر.
کەپوویەکی بەقۆرت توورە.
دەم و لێوێک وەک هەمیشە ئامادەبێ
ماچی خۆشەویستیی بکات.

96

Is Istanbul a cradle for sunlight?
Is it a station where exiles sleep?
Or is it a fishing net for the moon and a knife for the neck of stars?
Is Istanbul the gate of rain?
Or the city of locusts and the Sultan's sword?
Is Istanbul a breeze? Is it calm? Is it balm?
Or is it salt for the migrating pains of lovers?
Nali comes from there and brings Sharezur with him.

[...]

When he arrives I will tell him: My lord!
You leader of the army of sigh and pain!
Don't worry, even after you the army of our sorrow
is strong and successful.
We haven't been defeated after you. Why should we be?
When happiness is so weak and scared,
why should we be?
When pleasure is so easily
defeated by the attack of our catastrophe!

[...]

Now I mix my words in poetry's cup,
I mix dreams, nature, sounds and colour.
I paint the picture of Nali like this:
a face glowing with torment and scars,
or a fog mixed with the day's last light.
Two bright eyes, deep inside them the pebble of imagination is
    glowing,
they are two glittering balls inside two deep sockets,
their vision is sharp and quivering.
On the top, two thin eyebrows, connected in the middle,
are carrying the prayer stone of a forehead
where rain, flower and poetry pray.
Two cheeks full of runnels,
scarred by the years' ploughing,
and falling under thick shadows.
A crooked nose, angry.
Lips that seem to be always ready
to kiss a loved one.

ڕەنگی قژی تاریك و ڕوون.
دەست و پەنجەی بچووك بچووك مندااڵنه.
دەنگی: هێور... وەختێئەدوێ
دەستیش ئەبن به جۆلانه و بەپاڵەكانی ئاخاوتن
دێن و ئەچن.
كه شیعر ئەخوێنێتەوه، له گەڵیا ئەچەمێتەوه
وەكوو سوجده بۆ زمانی كوردیی بەرێوایه.
پاڵێك[40] و ڕیشی تێكەڵاو
سنووریان زەردیی دووكەڵه.
دەمارەكانی پشتی دەست
وەك جۆگەلەی باریك و شینی سەر نەخشەن.
له زۆر كەس بااڵی كورتره.

[...]

بەڵێنه هەر ئەم شەو درەنگان له كەنار
ئەو گۆمه غەمگینەی تەنیشتمان
دوو قوڵیی یەكتری ببینین
ئەزانم هەر كه هات.. پێم ئەڵێ:
– ئەستەموولا دەشتی خوێو
برینم ڕێبواری پێپەتی سەر ئەوه
من گەڵا ئاخێكی وەریوم
ڕەشەبای مەوسیمی فیراقیش هەر ئەمبا و
ئاشییان به تەنها قەڵەمی بێخەوه!

ڕەفیقان! بەڵام ئەز هەتاكوو
ئەم ئاشی غوربەت و حەسرەته ڕمهاڕێ
خەیاڵی حوزوری لای ئێوەم وردتره.
ئەم بادەی بەهەشتی سوراحی گەردنەم
تا هیجرەت كۆنی كات
بۆ نەسلی قەسیدەی داهاتووم
نۆشینی خۆشتره.
عەزیزان! لەكوێ بم
تانجەرۆ ئاوێنەی پێش بووكی بەیازمەو
چاوانی "حەبیبه"یش كەوسەرمه!
لێی ئەچمەوه پێششەوەو ئەپرسم:
– سەروەرم!
كەی شیعر بەسەرتا ئەبارێو
ئازارت تەر ئەكات؟

[40] پاڵێك: موی سمێڵ كه تێكەڵ به ڕیش ئەبێ.

The colour of his hair a mix of light and dark.
His hands are small, small like children's.
His voice: calm… when he talks
his hands become swings and move
with the pace of words.
When he reads his poetry, he bends
as if bowing to Kurdish language.
His moustache blends with his beard,
their border goldened by smoke.
The veins on the back of his hands
are like thin, blue rivers on a map.
He is shorter than most people.

[…]

It is planned that later tonight by the shore
of the sad pond next to us
the two of us meet.
I know when he comes he will tell me:
"Istanbul is a salt field
and my wound is a barefoot passenger, walking it.
I am a fallen leaf-sigh,
the wind of the parting season keeps taking me
and my only home is my sleepless pen.

My dear friends! As long as
the mill of exile and frustration grinds me
my attention to you is sharper.
The more exile ages this heavenly wine of my neck's jug
the better it is to drink
for the next generation of my verse.
My dear ones! Wherever I may be,
Tanjero lake is the mirror before my white papers' bride,
the eyes of Habiba are my Kauser."
I will get close and ask him:
"My lord!
When does poetry rain on you,
when does it wet your pain?"

– ئەو فەسڵەی کە عیشق ئەبێتە ئاسمانم
ئەو دەمەی کە سەرم
چەخماخە ئەدات و
ژان ئەبێبە هەورم.

[...]

– ئەی باشە سەروەرم! کەی هاتی؟ چۆن هاتی؟
"سالم"ت نەبینی
پێش ئەوەی کۆچ بکەیت؟!

– لەبیرمە ئەو سوبحی پایزەی کۆچم کرد
منیش وەك نارەوەن ئەوەریم.
بەیانییەم غوروبی وەسلم بوو
ئاگربووم لەسەرمای فیراقدا ئەلەرزیم
بەرێوە کولۆکۆم بردە لای
"سالم"ی نەسیمی شارەکەم
گریانم ماچی کرد، خەزانم باوەشی پێداکرد
لەبیرمە پێی وتم: رەفیقی رۆحەکەم!
وێڵاشی تەنیاییەم
بەم وەرزی ناوەختەی چاورێزان بەرەو کوێ؟
بەرەو کوێچاوەکەم،
رووی ژیلەی خۆم تێکرد:
"ئازیزی ئازیزان!
چارەنووس رێبواری رێی هات و نەهاتەو
نازانم هودهودی ئەم رۆحەم
بەرەو کوێئەفڕێت و کام کونجی غەریبی
ئەبێتە هێلانەم.
نازانم مەوجێکم سەری خۆم لە خۆڵدا هەڵ ئەگرم.
شیعرێکم تلاوتل ئەرۆم و درەختم باڵا ئەگرم.
"سالم"ی هەناسەم! ئەرجوی من هێندەیە:
کە جارجار ئەستێرەی کشاوی یادی من
لە خەونی قەسیدەی جوانتانا ببینن"
ئەوەندە و رۆیشتم و لەولای "وەیس" بەولاوە
بۆ دواجار ئاوڕم لە چاوی جێماوم دایەوە
ئاوڕێلەوساوە: شەوگاری هیجرەتم
گۆچانی تاریکیی دایە دەست غوربەتم.

100

"The season when love becomes my sky,
when my head starts lightning
and pain becomes my cloud."

[...]

"But my lord! When did you come? How did you come?
Didn't you meet Salem[47]
before you started your journey?"

"I remember the autumn morning when I departed,
I was autumning like the elm tree.
My morning was the sunset of togetherness.
I was fire, shivering in the cold of parting.
I took my embers to the breeze of my city, to Salem.
My tears kissed him, my autumn hugged him.
I remember he told me: you friend of my soul
placenta of my loneliness!
Where are you heading in this untimely season of fall?
Where are you heading, my precious eyes?
I faced him with my embers:
'My dearest!
Fate is travelling a dangerous path.
I don't know where this soul's hoopoe
is flying to and which corner of exile
will become my nest.
I am a wave heading to dry lands,
a poem rolling, a tree flying.
Salem of my breaths! My wish is only this:
to see the shooting star of my remembrance
in the dream of your beautiful verse.'
That was all I said and then I left.
After Weis, I turned back for the last time
to look at my left behind eyes.
Since then the nights of my migration
have given a cane of darkness to my exile."

[47] Salem (in Kurdish: Salim) was a famous poet of the same generation
as Nali. They were good friends and wrote poems to each other
while Nali was in exile.

"لێرەدا پێی ئەڵێم: گەورەی من!. ڕێم ئەدەی تامنیش
ئەو شیعرنامەیەی کە دابووم بە هەمان -باد-ی تۆ، بەهەمان
پەیکی تۆ!، تایبەت بۆ چەندان "ساڵم"ی شارەکەم
شارەکەت، نیشانی تۆیشی بەم؟.. ڕێم ئەدەی؟ گوێت لێبێ؟
بەڵام من سەروەرم! ئەزانم کە گوێی تۆ، چاوی تۆ،
نا ئاشنان بە زەنگ و بەوێنەی زایەڵە و تان و پۆی
ئەم جۆرە شیعرانە! وتت چی.. سەروەرم؟، دڵنیام ئەو ئەڵێ:
"ناسکبێو خەیاڵی تیا بفڕێ.. حەزئەکەم گوێم لێبێ".

"ساڵم"ەکانی وڵاتی خەندەی گریاو!
ئەی کەشتیەکانی نێو تۆفان!
هاوڕێیان!
لە بەندەری تەمومژی ئەم کۆچەوە
کە شەوتانی بەئەستێرە و شیعر و زام و
چیرۆکەوە کردۆتە کۆڵ.
لەم بەندەری غوربەتەوە ئەتانبینم:
لە نێڕینەی زەریایەکی ترسا
لەگەڵ نێڕە نەهەنگێکی شێتا
کە مێژووی لیخن کردووە و
ئێسکی خۆڕەتاو ئەکرۆژێو
جوانیی ئەخوا...
ئەتانبینم: هێشتا لەسەر تەوقی سەری
وەکوو چاوتان، وشەتان پڕیشك ئەهاوێو
دەنگتان گڤەی هەڵکردنی هەر پێماوە.
ئەتانبینم: چرای ستوونی قەڵەمتان وەك گەردنتان
گەش ئەسووتێو
چارۆگەی هیوای سپیتان نەژاکاوە.
ئەی کەشتیەکانی نێو تۆفان!
لەم بەندەرە لمینەوە
کە ڕوناکیی ئازارتانی تنۆك تنۆك هەڵمژیوە
ئەتانبینین: حووتی تۆفان بەدەم باداوەی زەردەوە
ئەتانبات و ئەتانهێنێو
وەك لاشیپانی کەشتیتان
دەرگای لەشتان شەقەشەقی پێئەکەوێو
بەڵام لوتکەی بەجریوەی گیانی شینتان
وەك باڵاتان ڕێك وەستاوە.
ئەتانبینین: لەناو ئابلووقەی نێزەدا
سەرتان "دم دم"ی تازەیەو

102

Here I tell him, "My lord! Will you allow me
to show you the poem which I had given to your gentle wind,
to your same messenger! So that it gives it to the many Salems
of my city, your city? Will you allow me? Will you hear it?
But my lord! I know that your ears, your eyes
are unfamiliar with the voice, image and fabric of these poems.
What say you, my lord?" I am sure he will say:
"Let it be delicate, where imagination flies… I want to hear it!"

"Salems of the country of crying laughter!
You, ships inside the storm!
My dear friends!
From this misty harbour of exile
which carries on its shoulders
your nights with its stars, your poems, pains and stories,
from this harbour of exile I see you:
in the depth of fear's ocean
you are facing a crazy killer whale
who muddies history,
chews the bones of sunlight
and eats beauty.
I see that sitting on his head
your eyes sparkle like your words.
Your voice has retained the roar of a rising wind.
I see you: the lanterns of your pens, like your necks
are burning bright
and the sail of your white hope is not ruined.
You, ships inside the storm!
From this sandy harbour
that has absorbed the light of your pains drop by drop
we can see how the storm's whale
swings you in the yellow whirls
and like the anchor of your ship
the doors of your bodies start shivering
but the singing peaks of your blue souls
remain straight like your bodies.
We can see you: in the blockade of spears,
your heads are the new Dimdim castle

خانی لەپ زێڕینی وشەیش
قوللەی خامەی ئەم زمانەی بەرنەداوە.

"ساڵ"ەکانی وڵاتی خەندەی گریاو!
ئەی کەشتیەکانی نێو تۆفان!
هاوڕێیان!
تا ئەم تۆفانی نەهەنگە
کرنووشی نیشتنەوە ئەبا بۆ زەمین و
هەتا تاریکیی ئەوەرێ.
هەتا کەشتیەکانتان ئەیکەن بە جەژنی ئاو
هەتا بەندەرمان ئەیکەن بە جەژنی کەشتیی
ئەبێبانگی سەری ئێمە "نەو" و
سەوڵەکانی دەستی ئێوەیش "نەو" و "نەو"بێ
"ساڵ"ەکانی وڵاتی خەندەی گریاو!
هاوڕێیان!
ئالەم تاقە وشەیەدا
دوا ڕۆژ هەناسە ئەدات و
هەر لەم تاقە وشەیشدا
خەون هەڵدێ"!

[...]

- سەرەوەرم! دۆزەخی ئەستەموولا
هیچ لالە شیعرێکی تیا نەرواو!؟
دەریاچەی ئەو خەونە هیچ گەرا ئەستێرەی جێنەهێشت؟
قەتارەی ئەو هەووری وشانە نەخرۆشان؟
گزنگیان دانەرشت؟
بۆ جارێک، هەر جارێک، لەو ئاسکی شیعرانە
یەکێکیان ئەگەیشتنە لای ئێمە!؟

- ئاخر چۆن بسووتێم.. ڕۆشن نیم؟
ئاخر چۆن هەڵوەرێم.. پایزی شیعرنیم؟
ئاخر چۆن شارەزوور.. هەوورم بێت
سێڵاوی وشەنیم؟
ئاخر چۆن "حەبیبە" ئاسکم بێت
من دەشتی پاراوی خەیاڵا و بەستەنیم؟
کەم بووە شەوانە خەم نەزڕۆ
ئەستێرەی شیعرێکی لێنەبێ!.

104

and Khani lep-Zereen[48] of the words
has not left this language's pen.

You Salems of the country of crying laughter!
You ships in the storm!
My dear friends!
Until this storm of whale
bows to the land,
until darkness descends,
until your ships celebrate water,
until our coasts celebrate ships,
the clamour of our heads must be: No,
the paddles in your hands must remain: No and No.
You Salems of the country of crying laughter!
My dear friends!
Only in this single word
the future breathes,
only in this single word
dream rises!"

[...]

"My lord! Did any tulips of poetry
grow in the hell of Istanbul?
Did the ocean of that dream leave behind any star eggs?
Did the caravan of those words' clouds not stir?
Did they not shine? For once, only once,
why didn't one of poetry's gazelles reach us?"

"Is it possible to blaze without being bright?
Is it possible to fall without being poetry's autumn?
Is it possible that Sharezur becomes my cloud
without making me a flood of words?
Is it possible for Habiba to be my gazelle
without my becoming the lush field of imagination and verse?
Few nights did sorrow not give birth to a poem star.

[48] Amir Khan Lepzerin (in Kurdish: Emîr Xan Lepzêrîn) was a Kurdish
prince who ruled over Bradost and Urmia. At the beginning of the 17th
century, he tried to gain independence from the Ottomans and Persians
but was defeated in 1610 when the Safavids captured the Dimdim castle
and massacred everyone who defended it.

کەم بووە ڕۆژانە من نەبم بە هەڵم و
دانەکەم بۆ شەوێ!

زیاتر لێی ئەچمە پێشەوە. بۆ مژینی خەمی سپی
خۆشەویستیم ئەبێبە هەنگ، ڕیشی بە باخ.
زیاتر لێی ئەچمە پێشەوە، هێواش هێواش،
هەردوو کۆترە ساردەکانی دەستی ئەگرم،
هەر بەدەم گمەی شیعرەوە ئەیانخەمە
ناو سنگمەوە. بە گریان دایان ئەپۆشم.
هەوڵیش ئەدەم زەینی خۆم بکەم بە ماسیی،
بۆ ئەو بەحرەی لەبەردەمما دانیشتووە.
هەوڵیش ئەدەم تەماشام بکەم بە بەران
بۆ ئەو کێوەی بەرامبەرم ڕاوەستاوە.
دواتر ئەدوێم. ئەبم بە چیمەنی قسە،
بە چوار دەورا ئەتەنمەوە. ئەوسا ئیتر
بەدرێژیی باسی شارو هەناسەکانی بۆ ئەکەم.
باسی سووڕانەوەی مێژووی خوێنی بە دەوری
کوردا بۆ ئەکەم. حیکایەتی بێکۆتایی
"ڕیس و خوری"ی تفەنگەکانی بۆ ئەکەم.
باسی "تاقمی مومتاز"ی قوربانیەکانی بۆ ئەکەم.
شەڕی نێوان سەری خۆم و دەستی خۆمی
بۆ باس ئەکەم. ڕووناکیی بۆ ئەگێڕمەوە.
تاریکیی بۆ ئەگێڕمەوە.
ئینجا تۆزێئەچمە دواوە. ئەو ماچانە و
دیوانە تازەکەی خۆی و ئەو کۆڵەباڵەی
بە دیاری "مەلا عەبدولکەریمی مودەڕیس"[41]
بۆی ناردبوو، ئەیان پێچم لە ڕێحانەی
"بیار"ەوە و لەسەر ڕانی بۆی دائەنێم.
ماچەکان ئەخاتە سەرچاو. پڕ بە گیانی
ئاوارەیی بۆنی ڕێحانەکان ئەکات. هەر لەوێدا
کۆڵە باڵیش لەبەرئەکات. دیوانەکە ئەکاتەوە
دەستێک بە ڕیشیا ئەهێنێ. ڕووم تێئەکات و
پێم ئەڵێ"ئەم پیرەیشمان چیایەکە وەک
"شنرۆێ".. واصلیکە عەبیری سەلامم
بەو و پێشی بڵێلە دڵمایە وەک تانجەرۆ"
لەپاش تۆزێهەڵئەسین و ئەیبەم، ئەچین،

[41] مەلا عەبدولکەریم: "مەلا عەبدولکەریمی مودەڕیسی بیارەیی" زانای ئاینینی و نووسەری ناودار.

Few days did I not become a mist
and rain in the night."

I get closer to him. My love becomes a bee
to suck white sorrows,
his beard becomes a garden.
I get even closer, slowly slowly
I grab the cold doves of his hands
and put them inside my chest with cooing poetry,
I cover them with tears.
I try to make my mind a fish
for the ocean that is sitting before me.
I try to make my sight a ram
for the mountain standing before me.
Later I speak. I become the grass of conversation
extending in every direction. Then
I tell him all about the city and its breaths.
I will tell him about the history of blood
circling around the Kurds. I will tell him the endless story
of the warp and woof of weapons.
I will tell him about the brilliant group of victims.
I will tell him about the war between my head and my hand.[49]
I will tell the story of light,
the story of darkness.
Then I will go back a little. I put together the kisses,
his new collection, the Kulebal jacket
which Mullah Abdulkarimi Mudaris[50] had sent to him
and wrap them in Biyara's basil and put them on his lap.
He will put the kisses on his eyes.
As far as his exiled breath goes, he smells the basil.
Just then he wears the Kulebal. He will open the book
and touch his beard. He will face me and say,
"This old man is a mountain, like Shinirwe,
give him my scented regards and tell him
he is in my heart like Tanjero."
After a while we get up and I take him,

---

[49] Referring to the Kurdish civil war.
[50] Mullah Abdulkarimi Mudaris (in Kurdish: Mela Ebdulkerîmê
Muderîs) was a poet, writer and translator who died in 2005.

بەگوڵزارەکەی "مەسعود"[42]دا سوڕێك ئەخۆین.
چاوم لێیە لە هەندێ شوێن دائەنەوێ و
بۆنی گوڵەکانی ڕائەمێنێ، لە سەرتڵێ[43]
قسەکانی، شاگوڵێکیان ئەکاتەوە ئەیخاتە بەر
پشتێنەکەی، ئاوڕم لێئەداتەوە، پێئەکەنێت و
پێم ئەڵێ"ئەم باخەوانە تێم ئەگات!"

[...]

بەڵێنە هەر ئەمشەو لەکەنار
ئەو گۆمە غەمگینەی تەنیشتمان
دوو قۆڵیی یەکتری ببینین:
من: نالیی، حەزرەتی غەریبان ئەبینم
ئەو شەوە لە گزنگ موتوربە کراوە ئەبینم
ئەو کێوە کۆچەرە ئەبینم.
ئەو کە هات وەك ئاوو، کە گەیشت وەك تیشك و
کە هەڵنیشت وەکوو باز
من وەکوو خەیاڵی شارەزوور لێی ئەچمە پێشەوە.
هەر خێرا، هەواڵی گرنگی چەند سەرووی دەربەدەر..
هەواڵی گۆڕانیی وەکوو خۆی ترافیە.[44]
هەواڵی بەفری شێت لە دووریی هەڵکۆك.
هەواڵی چەند زاری هیلالی وەکوو خۆی ئەدەمێو
پێی ئەڵێم:
– سەروەرەم! بەرلەوەی تۆ بگەیت، لەوێبووم،
لە "جونێف". ڕۆژنێکیان لە جادەی ژمارە 1898.
لە کۆشکی نسرم و شێداری مێژودا، پلیکەی پێشینی
تەختەبەند. پلیکەی ڕۆژگاری پێچاوپێچ. بە کونی
هەتاودا، بردمیە ژێر خانێ، لەوێدا چاوم کەوت،
بەیەکەم ڕەوڕەوەوەی زمان و بەیەکەم قوتیلکەی
ناو ژووری شەوەزەنگ. لەوێبوو، هەر خۆی بوو.
"جەلادەت بەدرخان" –بەر لەمن ئەتناسێو باوەشێ
ماچیشی بۆ ناردووی..
من کە دیم شاخێبوو ئارەقی سەردێڕ و ستوونی
ئەرشت و منارەی وشەبوو، ئەسووتاو بەپێوە
وەستابوو، من کە دیم هەوورێکی ڕیشدار بوو

---

[42] مەسعود: "مەسعود محەمەد جەلی زادە" ڕووناکبیر و نووسەر و توێژەرەوەی ناسراو.
[43] سەرتڵ: هەڵبژێردراو لە هەرە باش.
[44] ترافیە: ئاوارە، دەربەدەربوو.

we go, we will circle the garden of Mas'ud[51].
I see him bending down in certain places
to smell his flowers. He considers his words,
chooses the best flower and puts it in his belt
then he turns around, smiles and tells me:
"This gardener understands me."

[…]

It is planned that tonight by the shore
of the sad pond beside us
the two of us meet:
I will meet Nali, the king of exiles.
I will meet that night grafted with dawn light.
I will meet that fleeing mountain.
He comes like water, arrives like light,
and lands like an eagle.
I will approach him like the thought of Sharezur.
Quickly, I will tell him the news of some displaced cypresses,
of songs exiled like himself,
of snow crazed by separation from the primrose.
I will give him the news of a few crescent moons like himself
and I will tell him:
My lord! Before you arrive, I was there
in Geneva. One day on the 1898 street,
in the old, damp castle of history with its front wooden stairs.
The spiral stairs of the days took me
through the hole of sunlight to a cellar.
There I saw the first stroller of language
and the first oil lamp of darkness's room.
He was there, it was him,
Jeladet Badir Khan[52], he knows you before me.
He sent you an embrace of kisses.
When I saw him he was a mountain sweating line brakes
and columns. He was the minaret of words,

---

[51] Mas'ud Muhammed (in Kurdish: Masud Mihammed) was a Kurdish writer, historian and linguist who died in 2002.
[52] Jeladet Bedir Khan (in Kurdish: Celadet Bedir-Xan) was a journalist and politician during the Ottoman empire.

به تەنها ئەیگرمان.
من وتم:
- سڵاو ئەی
ڕۆژنامەی باپیرە گەورەمان
لەگەڵ چی خەریکی؟!
ئەو وتی:
- خەریکم بە وشە
دیواری تاریکیی کون ئەکەم
ئەگەڕێم بۆ هەتاو.
- بەکونی هەتاودا من هاتم. وام پێوت.
ئەو وتی:
- باش هاتووی!
تۆ شیعری کام شاری؟!
من وتم:
- هی نالیی!
ئەو وتی:
- ئاخ! نالیی
دوو زام و دوو کسپەو
دوو ئاخی چەند لەیەك نزیکین
هەر ئەڵێی جمکی ئەم غوربەتەین
ئەی هیچت لەگەڵ خۆت هێناوە
بۆ شەوی غەریبیم؟!
من پێم وت:
- مۆمێکی ئەشکەوتی باڵەکیان..
یەکەمین ڕۆژنامەی بارانی ئەیلوڵ هێناوە
من "دەنگی پێشمەرگە"م
لەگەڵ خۆم هێناوە.
ئەو وتی:
- ڕۆژنامە! پەنجەرەی دەنگمانە
ئەو وەختەی کە بەسەر دنیادا ئەڕوانێ.
ئەوەتا من لێرە یەکەمین پەنجەرەم کردەوە.
تیلچافە[45] ڕێوبانی هەنگاومان.
سەیرکە! چواردەوورم بەناسۆر گیراوە
هەر حەرفە و هاوارم لێئەکاو
نامۆییش دڕك و داڵ!.
خۆش هاتیی!
دیارییەکەت ئەوەمەو
خۆزگەم بوو بیبینم.

45 تیلچاف: شەوەزەنگ ئەمووستەچاو.

110

blazing, standing up.
When I saw him he was a bearded cloud
roaring on his own.
I said:
"Salam to you, our great-grandfather newspaper!
What are you up to?"
He said:
"I am about to pierce the wall of darkness
by words,
I am searching for sunlight."
"I came through the hole of sunlight," I told him.
He said,
"Good job you have come!
Which city's poem are you?"
I said:
"Nali's"
He said:
"Oh, Nali!
We are two very close wounds,
two pains, two sighs.
As if we are twins of this exile.
Have you brought anything
for the nights of my exile?"
I told him:
"I have brought you a candle from the Balekian cave,
the first paper in the September rain –
I have brought you *Dengi Peshmarga*."[53]
He said:
"Newspaper is the window of our voice
when you inspect the world.
I opened the first window here.
The path we step is darkness.
Look! I am surrounded by disappointment,
every letter is calling to me
and exile is like thorn-land!
Welcome!
Your present is my grandchild,
I was hoping to see it."

[53] The *Voice of Peshmarga* was a newspaper published in the 1970s by the
PUK party in the Kurdish mountains.

ئەزانم کە ناڵیی ئەو کاتە، کەژێکە لە بنار تا لووتکەی
هەر گوێیەو هەر چاوە. ئەزانم ئەیەوێبزانێ، ئەستێرەی
فرزەندی لانەواز لە کوێن و جریوەی غوربەتیان لەکام لا
رژاوە. بۆیە من هەر ئەدوێم:
– سەرەرەم! هەرەوەها لەولایش بووم. لە پاریس،
پاریسی بە شیعر پاراو و بە هزر چراخان. شەوێکی
تەمومژ بەدەوری مێژوودا باپووسکەی [46] پرسیار بووم
هەر خۆڵم ئەخواردو وێڵبوونم ئەپرسی:
– شەریف پاشا سەعید خەندان
شەقامی میسین ژمارە 20؟
"ئەمیشیان بەر لە من ئەتناسی و بەمندا دوا دەقی
یاداداشتی هاواری زامی خۆی بۆ ناردووی"
سەرەتا ئەچوومە بەردەمی هەرکەسێ، سەرێکی بائەدا:
"ببوورە ناوی وانایەتە خەیاڵم.."
یان ئەیوت: "پێم وابێشەقامی "میسین"یش بەرجادە کەوتبێ
نەمابێ.. نازانم.."
ئەمپرسی و ئەمپرسی و ئەرۆیشتم
باگژەی سۆراخ بووم.
خۆم لەگەڵ خۆم خۆم ئەدوام:
"من ئەبێلووتکەکان وێڵ نەکەم
بۆ ئەوەی بچمەوە سەرچاوەی بەرزایی
من ئەبێشوورەکان وێڵ نەکەم
بۆ ئەوەی بگەمە سەرەتاو کۆتایی"
تا دوایی شەقامێبردمیە بەر کۆشکی کتێب و رۆژنامە فرۆشێ.
کۆشکەکە بێهودە ئەیرواینیە دەوروبەر وەک "رامبۆ"!.
کۆشکەکە لە ماڵی نەهێنینی گوێ چەمی "مانگ" ئەچوو.
خاوەنی کۆشکەکە... درێژ و رەقەڵە
هەر ئەتەووت خاوەنی "شەبەنگە بەرۆژە" [47]
ئەدەرسم دایە دەست. چاویلکەی هێنایە سەر لووتی.
دوای کەمێبە پەنجە ئاماژەی بەرەوڵای گردێکی ڕوتەڵە بۆ کردم.
پێی وتم:
– ژەنەراڵ؟! ئەناسم
هەموو رۆژ رۆژنامەم لا ئەکڕێ
هەر لە دوای کۆنگرەی ئاشتی بوو
لە خانووی شەقامی "میسین"یش دەریانکرد!

---

[46] باپووسکە: کڕێوەی بەفر بە باوە.
[47] خاوەنی شەبەنگە بەرۆژ: مەبەست لە نووسەری ناسراو و خواڵێخۆشبوو (شاکیر فەتاح)ە کە بە دەستی ڕژێمی
عێراق شەهیدکرا.

I know that at this stage Nali is a mountain,
top to toe ears and eyes. I know that he wants to know
where the homeless children's stars are
and where their singing exile has been spilt.
This is why I keep talking:
"My lord! I was also over there, in Paris.
The Paris which is lush with poetry and bright with intellect.
On a misty night I was a snowstorm of questions, circling history.
I kept circling and my search kept asking:
'Sherif Pasha Saeed Khendan[54],
Number 20, Missin Street?'
(He too knows you before me and with me
he sent you the last manuscript
of his wound's scream.)
At first, whoever I asked would shake his head and say:
'Sorry, I can't remember such a name.'
Or they would say: 'I believe Missin street has been abolished,
maybe it is not there any more… I don't know.'
I asked and asked and walked
I was the wind of searching.
I was talking to myself:
'I must not lose the mountain-peaks
so that I can return to the source of height.
I must not lose the forts
so that I arrive at the beginning and the end.'
Until a road took me to the kiosk of a newspaper seller:
The kiosk was pointlessly looking at its surrounding like Rimbaud.
The kiosk looked like the moon's secret house by the river.
The owner of the kiosk was tall and thin
he looked like the writer of *Shebenga Beroj*[55].
I gave him the address. He put his glasses on his nose.
After a short while he pointed out a bare hill,
he told me:
'The General? I know him.
Every day he buys newspapers from me.
Just after the peace congress
they evicted him from the Missin Street address.

[54] Sherif Pasha Saeed Khendan (in Kurdish: Şerîf Paşa Seîd Xendan) was
a historian and politician, he represented Kurdish interests in the Treaty
of Serves which promised Kurdish independence.
[55] Shakir Fatah (in Kurdish: Şakir Fetah) was the writer of *Shebnge beroj*
(in Kurdish: *Şebenga Beroj*), he was killed by the Baath state.

لەوساوە کۆترێکی برسییه
لەوساوە، "پاریس"یش هێلانەی ولاتی لەبیرکرد!
داخەکەم! ژەنەرالا خەوونەکەی وەکوو خۆی
ئیستاکە لە ژوورێخزاوە تەنگ و تار،
داخەکەم! ولاتی ژەنەرالا
ئەسپێکی بێکەسە
لەدنیای ئەمرۆدا
کێحیلەی ئەبیسێ؟!

هەر رۆیشتم. هەتاکوو سۆراخی مەراقم گەیاندە ژوورەکەی.
ژوورێبوو بەقەم[48] بوو رەنگ و رووی.
بۆیرش[49] بوو هەناسەی.
غەمگین بوو، لە دیدەی تۆ ئەچوو، سەرورەم!. من کە دیم،
قەلەمی کۆماوەی ریش سپی. پلنگی پەککەوتە. خەریک بوو
بۆ جاری سەدەمین، یاددڵشتی بۆ دنیای کەرو کوێر ئەنووسی
ژوورەکەی سیخناخ بوو لە چاوی ئەبلەق بووی یاداداشت و
لەریزە تابووتی دۆسیییەی بەڵێنی دەولەتان. پربووپر،
لە چرە دووکەڵی دێهات و قریشکەی سێدارەی شەقامی نێو شاران
زەمانیمن لەلای دانیشتم. درەنگان شریتیی ڤیدیۆکەی
هەڵەبجەم دایە دەست. کەلێیدا. شاخی پیر،
زۆر گریا و ئەسرینی یاداداشتی داباری.
کە هەلسام پێی وتم:
– ئەم شەوی دۆزەخە
مەگەر هەر یەکێکی وەك نالیی
بیکاتە رەشماڵی شیعرێکی زۆر گەورە.

بەردەوام من زەمان ئەئاژوێم
ئەدوێم و
ناڵیش هەر گوێئەگرێلە هۆرەم
هەتاکوو پێی ئەلێم:
– وائیستەیش سەرورەم!
یەکەمین رۆژنامەی هەناسەی بەدرخان
یەکەمین یاداداشتی فرمێسکی خەندان و
یەکەمین رۆژنامەی چریکەی ئەیلوڵم
پێچاوە لەسەری برراوی "مارت"ەوەو
لەگەلا خۆم هێناوەمن
پێی ئەلێم:

---

[48] بەقەم: رەنگێنزوو کاڵ بێتەوە.
[49] بۆیرش: بۆنی شت کە لە جێی تەڕ دانراوە و شیی هەلهێناوە.

From then on he is a hungry dove,
from then on Paris made him forget the nest of homeland!
It is a shame! The general's dream, like himself,
is now squeezed into a tight dark room.
It is a shame! The general's country
is like a lonely horse in today's world,
who hears his neighs?'

I kept walking. Until my wandering worry reached his room.
It was a faded room, its breath smelt of damp.
It was sad, like your own eyes, my lord!
When I saw him, the crouching pen with grey beard,
the disabled tiger, was for the hundredth time
writing a memoir for the deaf and blind world.
His room was full of wide eyed memoirs
and coffins of the dossiers of the states' promises.
It was full of villages' smoke and gallows's screams from the city
    streets.
I sat by him for a while. Later I gave him the video of Halabja.
When he played it, the old mountain cried abundantly,
the tears of his memoirs flew.
When I got up he told me:
'Only someone like Nali
could turn this night of hell
into the black tent of a very great poem.'"

I continuously drive time.
I talk and Nali keeps listening to my song.
Until I tell him:
"And now my lord!
I have brought you the first paper of Bedir Khan's breath,
the first memoir of Khendan's tears,
and the first paper of September's song
wrapped around the decapitated head of March."
I will tell him:

115

– ده فەرموو لێم بگرە سەروەرم!
بۆ ئەوەی لەیەکتر دانەبڕێین!

[...]

ئەمشەو خەوێکم دێتە دی و نیشتمانم
لەناو دیدە و لەناو دەنگ و لەناو ڕیشی
نالیی دا دێ و ئەگاتە لام.
سنگم ئەبێتە "خاک و خۆڵا"
سەرم بەچوخمی "سەرشەقام"
ئەم شەو خەمێکم بەختیار.
مەراقێکم هێور، ئارام
ئەمشەو مندالییەم ئەبارێ
بەسەر یادی سەوزو سووردا و ئەمە دەربەندی پەپوولەو
دایکم ئەبن
بەمامزێسپی سپی و حیکایەتی "گردی ڕەش"یش
بەگرمەگرمی گەواڵەی هەووری سەرشار.

ئەمشەو خەمێکم بەختیار.
مەراقێکم پەل و پۆدار.
لەسووتاندا هەڵئەقوڵێم و
لەگریاندا سەوزم ئەکا "هەڵەبجە"ی یار.
ئەمشەو خەوێکم دێتە دی و ئەبم بە ئەسپێکی باڵدار
ئەمجارەیان من ناچمەوە لای نامۆیی و
شەو درەنگان هەر لە کەنار ئەو گۆمەوە
جلەو بۆ "با" شل ئەکەم و
لەگەڵا نالیی ئەرۆمەوە بۆلای "گۆیژە"و
پێکیشەوە ئەچینەوە لای "سالم"و
"حەبیبە"ی شار!

116

"Now take it from me, my lord!
So that we won't lose touch!"

[...]

Tonight one of my dreams will come true
and my homeland will come to me
through the eyes, voice and beard of Nali.
My chest will become Khakukhol[56],
my head the mew of Sersheqam.
Tonight I am a happy sorrow.
I am peaceful fascination.
Tonight my childhood rains
over the colourful memories
and I will turn into a butterfly valley.
My mother will become
a white gazelle and the story of Black Hill
will become the thundering clouds over the city.

Tonight I am a happy sorrow,
a fascination, lush with branches.
I am a fountain ablaze
and my beloved Halabja germinates me with her tears.

Tonight one of my dreams will come true
and I will become a winged horse.
This time I won't go back to exile
and late at night, just by the shore of that pond,
I will give free rein to the wind.
I will go back to Goyja mountain with Nali
and the two of us will go back to Salem,
to our Habiba, the city!

---

[56] Khakukhol (in Kurdish: Xakuxoll) is the village where Nali was born.

SHERKO BEKAS (in Kurdish: Şêrko Bêkes) was born on 2 May 1940 in Sulaymaniyah, Iraqi Kurdistan, the son of the Kurdish poet Fayak Bekas. In 1965, Bekas joined the Kurdish liberation movement and worked in the movement's radio station, The Voice of Kurdistan. He left his homeland because of political pressure from the Iraqi regime in 1986 and from 1987 to 1992, he lived in exile in Sweden. In 1992, he returned to Iraqi Kurdistan. He died of cancer in Stockholm, Sweden on 4 August 2013.

Bekas was a major poetic voice in Iraqi Kurdistan, being one of the first poets to break with the traditional rules of Kurdish poetry. Not only did he dispense with rhyme and introduce a new element known as 'Rûwange' (vision), but he also created the 'poster poem' in 1975. A two-volume collection of his complete poetic works in Kurdish was published in Sweden in 1990 / 1992.

Bekas' works have been translated into Arabic, Swedish, Danish, Dutch, Italian, French and English. In 1987, he was awarded the Tucholsky Scholarship of the Stockholm PEN Club and in the same year the Freedom of the City of Florence.

CHOMAN HARDI went to England as a refugee in 1993 and was educated at Oxford, London and Kent Universities. She returned to Kurdistan in 2014 to teach Literature and Gender Studies and founded the Center for Gender and Development Studies at the American University of Iraq-Sulaimani (AUIS). She has written about the impact of genocide on Kurdish women in Iraq, *Gendered Experiences of Genocide* (Routledge, 2011). Her English poetry collections, *Life for Us* (2004) and *Considering the Women* (2015), were published by Bloodaxe Books. *Considering the Women* received a Recommendation by the Poetry Book Society and was shortlisted for the Forward Prize.

Milton Keynes UK
Ingram Content Group UK Ltd.
UKHW040830030923
427816UK00012B/34